RICK .

He Who Has an Ear... Let Him Hear! (Foundations)

Jesus Pulled Me from the Grave
Then the Holy Spirit Blew Me Away

When my sister found me, I had no pulse, was not breathing, and I was cold! I had drunk an entire quart bottle of vodka on an empty stomach. That was fifteen years ago. Most of what I know about that day was told to me by my sister. With a blood alcohol level of 3.0, you do not remember much. They rushed me to the emergency room and immediately started intravenous therapy to flush the poison out of my system. The flushing took 13 hours, and I can safely say it was the worst day of my life. Yes, Jesus had to reach down and pull me out of the grave...a miracle for sure! True to His Word, Jesus took the worst day of my life and turned it into the best day of my life.

My recovery took ten years to complete, and during those years, I prayed one prayer over and over..."God, you heal me, you show me the way, and I will tell the world." As the tears of victory flow down my face, I know that the time has come to write this book and tell the world!

By reading this book, you will find out how I overcame 3 insane years (only by the Power of God) of crying myself to sleep nearly every night, crippling depression with suicidal thoughts. Additionally, you will learn how I overcame my drug and alcohol addiction, which had led to a huge chemical imbalance.

As great as that miracle was, it was only the tip of the iceberg. Regardless of whether you are a person running from the calling God has put on your life, a newly born-again Christian, or have been walking with the Lord for many years, this book contains fresh new revelations, many of which have not been exposed before.

These revelations came directly from the Holy Spirit, detailing how meditating on God's Word and the subsequent "Renewal of our Mind" actually transform our body's genetic chemical output leading to a life breathing with health and peace beyond understanding.

Revelation 2:7

To him who overcomes [the world through believing that Jesus is the Son of God], I will grant [the privilege] to eat [the fruit] from the tree of life, which is in the Paradise of God.

He Who Has an Ear, Let Him Hear

Trilogy Christian Publishers A Wholly Owned Subsidiary of Trinity Broadcasting Network

2442 Michelle Drive Tustin, CA 92780

Manufactured in the United States of America

10 9 8 7 6 5 4 3 2 1

Library of Congress Cataloging-in-Publication Data is available.

ISBN: 978-1-63769-020-8

E-ISBN: 978-1-63769-021-5

This book is dedicated to:

The Glory of God...

With special thanks to Trinity Broadcast Network, the *best* television on the planet. *Without TBN, I would not be alive today! Thank you, Paul, Jan, Matt and Laurie and the Pastors below:*

Andrew Wommack
Creflo Dollar
Greg Laurie
James Merritt
Joseph Prince
Joyce Meyer
Michael Youssef
Steven Furtick
Perry Stone
John and Pam Antonucci
Charles Stanley
Irvin Baxter
Hagee Ministries
Jentezen Franklin
TD Jakes
Beth Moore
Ron Carpenter
Dr. David Jeremiah
Randal Ackland

Table of Contents

Introduction

When my sister found me, I had no pulse, was not breathing, and I was cold! I had drunk an entire quart bottle of vodka on an empty stomach. That was fifteen years ago. Most of what I know about that day was told to me by my sister. With a blood-alcohol level of 3.0, you do not remember much. They rushed me to the emergency room and immediately started intravenous therapy to flush the poison out of my system. The process took 13 hours, and I can safely say it was the *worst* day of my life. The next day I opened my Bible and tuned into TBN (Trinity Broadcast Network). Switching on and off between the two, I averaged 6 hours a day for the next three years! I was 52 years old when I died. Reflecting...I realize I now have over 15,000 hours of contact with the reading of God's Word.

My death was the straw that broke the camel's back and proved that God will meet you wherever you are at in life. My story began as I was a young child. In this book, I detail the amazing changes I experienced personally that transformed me from a child beaten by his father and a 15-year-old molested by his catechism teacher into a person with a gut-wrenching lifelong sense of worthlessness, anger issues, atheism, who smoked a joint every couple of hours every day for 34 years in a row, alcoholic for ten years, and divorced after 32 years of marriage. My death by alcohol poisoning produced a whole person again with an exceedingly abundant life full of peace. Yes, Jesus had to reach down and pull me out of the grave...a miracle for sure. True to His Word, Jesus took the *worst* day of my life and turned it into the *best* day of my life.

Obviously, I needed to make some serious changes in my life, and I needed to make them like yesterday. So, how does God's Word produce lasting change, and what is the science behind it? What does that really look like?

Answers to these questions have escaped believers and non-believers for thousands of years, including the Christians who have experienced significant changes in their life by accepting Jesus as their

Lord and Savior. Yes, you can change, but not without the power of the Trinity! The greatest testimony that the Bible is *not* a compilation of short stories written by men is the innumerable amount of people whose lives have been drastically changed by reading His ever relevant, life-breathing Words.

Ultimately, my complete recovery took ten years. During those years, I prayed one prayer over and over…"God, you heal me, you show me the way, and I will tell the world." As the tears of victory flow down my face, I know that the time has come to write this book and tell the world!

Even more importantly, along with my miracle, the Holy Spirit showed me the science behind those changes. As I mentioned above, it was not enough for me to just receive a miracle for myself. In the back of my mind, there was always this deep need to understand the process of change scientifically so that I could share it with everyone. The Holy Spirit's inspired wisdom focused on epigenetics, neurology, nutrition, and quantum physics.

Regardless of whether you are a person running from the calling God has put on your life, a newly born-again Christian, or you have been walking with the Lord for many years, this book contains fresh new revelations, many of which have not been exposed before. These revelations came directly from the Holy Spirit, detailing how meditating on God's Word and the subsequent "Renewal of our Mind" transform our body's genetic chemical output leading to a life breathing with health and peace like mine.

This book is the first in a series of three books I will be writing. In my second book, *Biblical Nutrition*, I will be showing you an extensive comparison between the world's philosophy of how to be healthy and God's method. The book will combine all we have learned in this book and expand on it, proving God's path to health is so much more effective and all-inclusive. In the book, I will be sharing the insights I was led to by the Holy Spirit regarding the effects of anxiety, stress, and traumatic life experiences. I will show you how these three create chemical imbalances.

The third book, *Death Spiral vs Life Spiral*, will be a summary of the first two books. In the third book, we will learn what Satan's neurological tree looks like and what God's neurological tree looks like. The book will have awesome graphs and illustrations to help you easily see the depth of Gods' love for us in a way you would have never imagined!

The unique insights imparted to me by the Holy Spirit (the true author of these books) will explain the physiology behind: meditating on God's Word, effects of our belief system, renewing our mind, achieving discernment (hearing God's Voice), the renewal and strengthening of our immune system and the healing properties of a body at rest. By the time you finish reading all three books, you will have a complete understanding of how the Trinity's transformative processes produce Their *ultimate* gift...a sense of *peace* beyond all understanding.

As the world rapidly approaches the end-times, the ability to change will become harder and harder to come by. The time is *now* to enter into a relationship with the Trinity and let Their transforming powers put a smile on your face that won't go away. The truths found in this book will provide you with a Biblical and scientific understanding of how God's Word changes us from the inside out, creating a supernatural defense against the powers of darkness. This will not only enable you to withstand the devil's onslaught, but it will also empower you to thrive, stay at peace, and maintain a state of rest.

Foundational Insights

I am now 67 years old, and if I have learned anything in life, it is this...nothing in life is coincidental. There is a reason why you have purchased this book. I do not profess to know the reason why, but you can be sure of this, after reading this book, you will see life in a different, exceedingly wonderful light.

If you are like me, there were many "light bulb" moments during my journey through life. Case in point: I distinctly remember when I turned 30 years old. I had a flashback to when I was 18 years old, standing in front of my parents, lashing out to them in response to lectures about how I was making bad choices. I confidently told them I knew all there was to know and how they were "just so wrong."

Well, now being 30 years old, I realized just how right they were... that was a hard pill to swallow. Effectively, I did not know what I did not know! When I turned 40 years old and looked back at being 30 years old, it happened again. The wisdom of having lived 40 years proved to be superior to the wisdom of 30 years. The same thing happened at 50 and 60 years old.

The point being, the older I get and accumulate more data, the more I realize just how much there is to know about life.

I said all that to frame these next words. Up until the moment I died at 52 years old, I lived what I would define as a normal life for a person who had limited Christian knowledge and no relationship with God, Jesus, and Holy Spirit. I never went to church and had no clue about the benefit of doing so.

I suffered from great emotional swings, heartbreaks, constant stress, and anxiety (normal, right?). I, not knowingly (did not know what I did not know), listened to all the wrong people...my so-called friends! If someone hurt me, I hurt them back. To say I was selfish and egotistical would be an understatement.

And...then I died!

As I mentioned in the introduction, the next day, I opened the Bible and tuned into Trinity Broadcast Network and have not looked back since. Talk about not knowing what I did not know! As I will detail later in the book, for the next ten years, the Holy Spirit took me from subject matter to subject matter. I had no clue where I was being taken.

To date, 15 years later, I not only see life from an entirely new perspective; I am the most emotionally stable and peaceful me I have ever been; I virtually have a smile on my face every day that rarely goes away. No pot, no alcohol, no medications...no anything. I literally cannot wait to wake up each morning to see what the day will bring.

If any of this has sparked your attention, please give me your eyes and ears for as long as it takes to read this book. You do not have to suffer as I did! *Please note*: God is no respecter of person, meaning it does not matter who you are or what you may have done in your life. He will do the same for you if you will give Him the time.

Okay, let us get back on track.

First, I will be defining foundational Biblical truths you will need to understand the hurdles to be overcome during the transitional process of change. Unlike a track star who jumps over the hurdles, running a high hurdle race, God will take you through the hurdles. Running the race this way is what produces long-lasting change.

Second, I will be providing the actual scientific evidence of how God's Word changes us mentally and physically.

Chapter One

Biblical Foundations

To impart to you the wisdom the Holy Spirit revealed to me regarding the physiological ways God's Word changes us from the inside out on a neurological level, we need to establish some foundational Biblical understandings. The Bible is a book containing a seemingly endless number of hidden mysteries.

My opinion is God wrote it this way to confuse the devil so he would not be able to expose God's plan of redemption.

The foundational Truths below are critical to understanding the neurological and physiological effects of reading God's Word.

You should consider referring to these Truths before reading each chapter to keep them fresh in your mind.

First foundational Truth: probably the most important Truth of all! The Bible was written both literally and symbolically. All events in the Bible are literal, but also symbolically, they represent a Spiritual Truth. Example: Egypt is a literal place where the Israelites were held in bondage and slavery until the Exodus, but symbolically it spiritually represents the state of mind (the thought life) of an unbeliever held hostage to sin with its negative neurological and physiological side effects of worthlessness, loneliness, disease, behavioral issues, depression, suicidal thoughts, alcohol/drug addictions to name but a few.

Key Point: Proportional to the degree of understanding a person has of the Trinity is the degree to which one obtains perfect health, a state of rest and peace beyond understanding. In other words, the power or effectiveness (ability to change and be healthy) is directly related to the strength of our relationship with the Trinity. Maybe it is best to say it this way: believers are very familiar with this Biblical quote, "The Truth Shall Set You Free," but ironically...it is only the truth that one knows that can set them free!

> Then you will know the truth and the truth will set you free.
>
> John 8:32 (NIV)

Second foundational Truth: it is in our nature to rebel! Parents have daily firsthand experiences with this aspect of our natural self. They learn very early on in a child's life that if you tell a child not to do something...guess what—that is the very thing they will do. This natural tendency is literally and symbolically documented in the book of Genesis.

The Fall of Man

> Now the serpent was more crafty (subtle, skilled in deceit) than any living creature of the field which the Lord God had made. And the serpent (Satan) said to the woman, "Can it really be that God has said, 'You shall not eat from any tree of the garden'?" And the woman said to the serpent, "We may eat fruit from the trees of the garden, except the fruit from the tree which is in the middle of the garden. God said, 'You shall not eat from it nor touch it, otherwise you will die.'" But the serpent said to the woman, "You certainly will not die! For God knows that on the day you eat from it your eyes will be opened [that is, you will have greater awareness], and you will be like God, knowing [the difference between] good and evil." And when the woman saw that the tree was good for food, and that it was delightful to look at, and a tree to be desired in order to make one wise and insightful, she took some of its fruit and ate it; and she also gave some to her husband with her, and he ate.
>
> Genesis 3:1-6 (AMP)

I find it very interesting that before Adam and Eve were banished from the Garden of Eden, they walked with God. God had not given them the Ten Commandments. He only gave them one commandment...to not eat from the tree of the knowledge of good vs. evil. Doing what children do best, they immediately ate from that tree.

The Holy Spirit unpacked this Truth beautifully and simplistically for me one morning while I was reading my Bible. Out of nowhere, the Holy Spirit said to me: "I want you to imagine ten three-year-old children playing in a park with no parents around. They are unique in the fact that they have never been taught the difference between right and wrong. They are all in a sandbox with five toys." Then the Holy Spirit asked me, "what do you think is going to happen?" Yup, it is not going to be pretty, they will surely fight over the toys because they were not taught right from wrong and were not supervised. Then the Holy Spirit said, "it is now lunchtime, and there is food on a table next to the sandbox, but there is only enough food to feed five of them." Then the Holy Spirit asked me, "what do you think will happen?" Yup, somebody is not going to eat.

Obviously, without a parent to supervise, the prevailing law of human life is the "law of the jungle": my toy—my food, and only the strongest will survive. So, if children must be supervised and corrected to become mature, stable adults, who was/is the originator of the lessons teaching us right from wrong?

On the surface, our initial response would be our immediate parents, but if that is true, then don't we need to go back in time from generation to generation...all the way back to Adam and Eve to find out who the originator was? If we are all born with the nature of the law of the jungle, how do we learn the difference between right and wrong?

Here is the *beautiful* part...God's Holy Spirit was, is, and will always be our parent who teaches not only right from wrong but also the value of taking the higher road...His road—the way of *Love*! If the children mentioned above were Adam and Eve (we all begin our relationship with the Trinity as children), then God as the parent would have been the one who said, "children, you should share your toys so *all* can have fun," and "children, you should share the food so *all* can eat."

Key point: we have two forces that battle against our ability to walk in Love and take the higher road...living life God's way. The first is our natural tendencies to act 100% selfishly, which by the way, leads to 100% lawlessness, i.e., my toys, I'm playing, you are not, my rules; and my food, I'm eating, you are not, my rules. The second is Satan's nature, which is to kill, steal, destroy, and deceive us into thinking his thoughts. Thinking the way Satan does also changes the body's genetic chemical output leading to a weakened immune system...allowing disease and mental illness to flourish, slowly killing us from the inside out.

> The thief comes only in order to *steal and kill and destroy*. I came that they may have life, and have it to the full.
>
> John 10:10 (NIV)

When a person accepts Jesus Christ as their savior, a process of change begins. Thinking the way Jesus does changes our body's genetic chemical output, progressively strengthening our immune system and transforming us from the inside out.

Surely, God has His hands full with the likes of us, but do not ever overlook this vital Truth...God is the only GOoD force in the universe looking out for our best interests. All that is GOoD in the world originated through Him and by Him!

Third foundational Truth: as believers, the mysteries of the Bible are *not* hidden *from* us; they are hidden *for* us.

Key Point: Exposing these amazing hidden mysteries requires a sincere desire to have a relationship with God, Jesus, and the Holy Spirit and a relentless determination to read His Word.

> This, then, is how you should regard us: as servants of Christ and as those entrusted with the mysteries God has revealed.
>
> 1 Corinthians 4:1 (NIV)

Fourth foundational Truth: God has never been impressed with a person's education or the lack thereof, status, or wealth. The only thing God searches for is the sincerity of one's heart.

> A person might think their own ways are right, But the Lord weighs the heart.
>
> Proverbs 21:2 (NIV)

For it is the sincerity of the "true" believer's heart that causes her/him to relentlessly study the Word of God pursuant to an honest and open relationship with the Trinity.

Key Point: Subsequently, it is the depth of our relationship with the Trinity which produces the changes the believer/unbeliever knows in their heart they need to make to walk in His peace and His rest in their life.

Fifth foundational Truth: We are wired for change, but we need to experience the fulness of the Trinity to effect that change. I have done a lot of research in this area and found Dr. Caroline Leaf to be one of the world's greatest authority on the brain's ability to change. Here is the About statement found on her website:

> Dr. Caroline Leaf is a communication pathologist and cognitive neuroscientist with a master's and PhD in Communication Pathology and a BSc Logopaedics, specializing in cognitive and metacognitive neuropsychology. Since the early 1980s, she has researched the mind-brain connection, the nature of mental health, and the formation of memory. She was one of the first in her field to study how the brain can change (neuroplasticity) with directed mind input.
>
> During her years in clinical practice and her work with thousands of underprivileged teachers and students in her home country of South Africa and in the USA, she developed her theory (called the

> Geodesic Information Processing theory) of how we think, build memory, and learn, into tools and processes that have transformed the lives of hundreds of thousands of individuals with Traumatic Brain Injury (TBI), Chronic Traumatic Encephalopathy (CTE), learning disabilities (ADD, ADHD), autism, dementia and mental ill-health issues like anxiety and depression. She has helped hundreds of thousands of students and adults learn how to use their minds to detox and grow their brains to succeed in every area of their lives, including school, university, and the workplace.[1]

Key Point: How is God's love demonstrated? What is the grace of Jesus? How does the Holy Spirit impart wisdom to us? Only when a person knows the answers to these questions will that person experience the fullness of the Godhead's healing power and its ability to change us from the inside out.

Sixth foundational Truth: Satan has been formulating his deceptions for a very long time (since the Garden of Eden). He learned along the way to adopt the "if you cannot beat them, join them" strategy. So, he devised methods to infiltrate the church to plant deceptive seeds within the minds of members of the congregations.

> And no wonder, since *Satan* himself masquerades as an angel of light.
>
> 2 Corinthians 11:14 (NIV)

Chapter Summary

The purpose of Chapter 1 was to provide enough Biblical foundational truth to help you understand what you may not have known, you did not know. These basic truths are essential to understand what you are fighting against to make long-lasting changes in your life. Spending time learning about the Trinity is the only path to true freedom in life and a peace beyond all understanding.

You can directly expedite your rate of change proportional to the number of hours you spend in the Word. All the while, you will be experiencing the neurological and physiological changes which subliminally occur when you accept Jesus as your Savior. The next step is to walk out (live by) what you have learned in your studies. This is a deeply hidden mystery within the Bible and will take some time and effort on your part for it to become clear. Your reward will be great...so hang in there!

In the next chapter, we will begin looking at individual concepts you need to understand to speed up the change process. Lucky you, by reading this book, you will learn in a very short time what it took me ten years to understand.

Chapter Two

Understanding the Symbology of the Tree of Life and the Tree of the Knowledge of Good/Evil in Genesis

This chapter will unpack both the literal and symbolic nature of trees as referenced within the Bible. An extremely important hidden mystery resides within the Biblical account of the two trees found in the Garden of Eden. The mystery of these trees needs to be unveiled to understand how God changes us from the inside out on a neurological level, which, in turn, changes our physiology.

Going back in history, we can see that trees have always been considered representative of life, power, prosperity, and wisdom. They are thought of as the witnesses of the creation due to their long life span.

As I mentioned in the introduction, I was given fresh new revelations by the Holy Spirit, and this is the first of many:

The Holy Spirit revealed an extremely important and rarely discussed visual to me; trees, with their associated branches and roots very closely resemble the neurological structures found in the human brain, central nervous system, and in our veins and arteries. Probably just a coincidence...no! Keep this visual in your mind as you read further. You will learn in Chapter 7 just how closely related the structure of a tree is to a neuro pathway.

> And [in that garden] the LORD God caused to grow from the ground every tree that is desirable and pleasing to the sight and good (suitable, pleasant) for food; the tree of life was also in the midst of the garden, and the tree of the [experiential] knowledge (recognition) of [the difference between] good and evil.
>
> Genesis 2:9 (AMP)

> So the Lord God took the man [He had made] and settled him in the Garden of Eden to cultivate and keep it. And the Lord God commanded the man, saying, "You may freely (unconditionally) eat [the fruit] from every tree of the garden; but [only] from the tree of the knowledge (recognition) of good and evil you shall not eat, otherwise on the day that you eat from it, you shall most certainly die [because of your disobedience]."
>
> Genesis 2:15-17 (AMP)

Literal Account of Genesis 2:15-17

- We see here the physical description of two different types of trees, each having its own type of fruit. According to the Bible, eating the fruit from the tree of life causes a person most certainly to live forever. Eating the fruit from the tree of the knowledge of good and evil causes a person most certainly to die.
- I find it extremely interesting that trees are used literally in the Bible more than any other living thing, excluding God and people. They are the oldest living things on our planet, surviving 10,000 years or more.
- Trees are likened to Jesus; they give and give just like He promises to do for us. They give life, beauty, and shade. They clean the air and hold back erosion. Additionally, they offer shelter, food, and protection. I find it compelling that trees are also associated with every major character found in the Bible.

Symbolic Account of Genesis 2:15-17

Are you ready to go deep? The symbolic meanings of the tree of life and its fruit are as follows:

Symbolically, fruit represents a state of mind, a way of thinking. So, when the Bible tells us they eat of the fruit from the tree of life, what they symbolically were doing was adopting the mindset of Jesus Christ, His way of thinking. This caused their bodies to function 100% positively, giving them the ability to live forever. Biblically, this state of mind is referred to as the law of the Spirit of Life.

Key point: The more Spiritual fruit we eat, in essence, the more we are buying into and believing in the highest Truth there is...the way of Love; the healthier and stronger we become. This is because the fruit from the tree of life is the entire Word of Jesus (life)!

> In the beginning was the Word, and the Word was with God, and the Word was God.
>
> John 1:1 (NIV)

> because throught Christ Jesus the law of the Spirit who gives life has set you free from the law of sin and of death.
>
> Romans 8:2(NIV)

> And this, so that I may know Him [experientially, becoming more thoroughly acquainted with Him, understanding the remarkable wonders of His Person more completely] and [in that same way experience] the power of His resurrection [which overflows and is active in believers], and [that I may share] the fellowship of His sufferings, by being continually conformed [inwardly into His likeness even] to His death [dying as He did].
>
> Philippians 3:10 (AMP)

> I assure you and most solemnly say to you, the person who hears My word [the one who heeds My message], and believes and trusts in Him who sent Me, has (possesses now) eternal *life* [that is, eternal life actually begins—the believer is transformed], and does not come into judgment and condemnation, but has passed [over] from death into life.
>
> John 5:24 (AMP)

The symbolic meanings of the tree of the knowledge of good vs. evil and its fruit are as follows:

Eating the fruit from this tree symbolically represents buying into the state of mind defined in the Bible as "The Law." Semantically, do good—get good! Do bad—get bad! Anything and everything that has to do with trying to earn salvation through our own efforts is considered works of the flesh and bring only death. Biblically, this state of mind is referred to as the Law of sin and death (our sinful nature).

Key point: The second we chose to know the difference between good vs. evil, we became torn apart mentally and spiritually separated from God (veiled). Effectively it became the origin of the "Battlefield of our Mind." Since then, Satan has been constantly deceiving us into believing in our 100% selfish and 100% lawless ways to save ourselves and the justification of harming others.

In Chapter 3, I will go into much greater detail showing how the stress and anxiety created by knowing the difference between right and wrong have been killing us from the inside out by altering the chemical output of our genes.

Chapter Summary

Prior to eating the fruit from the tree of the knowledge of good vs. evil, Adam and Eve only had one mindset, God's way of living and thinking, the way of *Love.* Because Adam and Eve only had God's mindset (oneness of thought), their mind did not torment itself. Effectively, they were in a mental state of complete and total rest. When the human body is in a state of rest, its metabolism, genetic chemical output, and immune system function at the highest level of efficiency.

Even during the time of Genesis, there were just as many germs and viruses that could have made Adam and Eve sick and die, yet the Bible says they lived more than 900 years. What changed? What eventually caused them to die? Theoretically, they could have lived forever, which was God's original plan. *Being double-minded!*

Even though the Ten Commandments were not given to man until around 1300 BC, simply knowing the difference between right and wrong not only separates us from having a relationship with God but begins the process of weakening our immune system due to condemnation, fear, stress, and anxiety. Here is the Bible account:

> Then the eyes of the two of them were opened [that is, their awareness increased], and they knew that they were naked; and they fastened fig leaves together and made themselves coverings.
>
> Genesis 3:7 (AMP)

> Then the man and his wife heard the sound of the Lord God as He was walking in the garden in the cool of the day, they hid from the Lord God among the trees of the garden.
>
> Genesis 3:8 (NIV)

Key point: here is why this chapter is so important! The biblical account tells that if we eat of the tree of the knowledge of good vs. evil, we will surely die.

Look at the graph below: vertically are the years people lived, and horizontally are years after banishment from the Garden of Eden. Please note these are estimates only and are only used for illustration purposes.

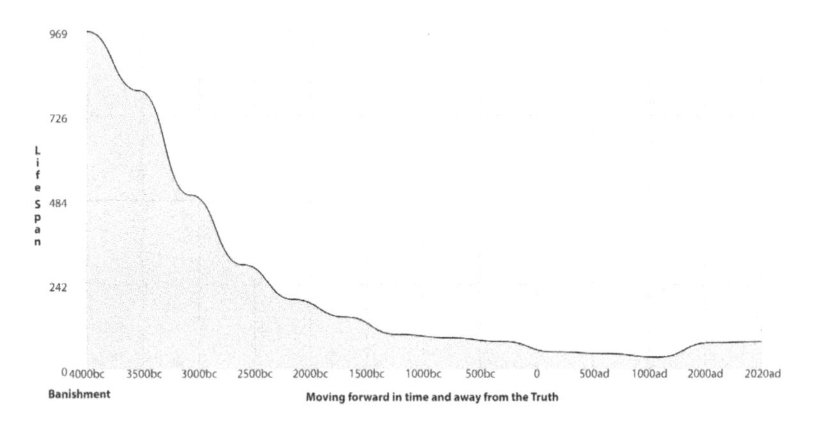

The start point is the moment when Eve and Adam ate the fruit and were banished from the garden of Eden. Remember, they now have two mindsets. So as time progressed (moved away from the truth) from the moment of banishment, look what happened to our life expectancy.

The physiology of 1,000 years without a Bible.

If we look closely at the graph, at the time of AD 500 to AD 1500, we see the lowest life span. This period is called the Middle Ages. The first 500 years of this period is known as the "Dark Ages." If you know your history, what was unique about that period was the lack of a readable Bible leading to the world almost losing its hold on Biblical truth. Also, the black plague occurred during this time. Point being: no Bible, no truth...no *life*! The average lifespan during this period was 35–40 years. Probably just a coincidence!

Chapter Three

The Negative Neurological and Physiological Effects of Living with Two Natures

Prior to entering into a relationship with God, Jesus, and the Holy Spirit, I did not realize I was being whispered to by the devil and definitely had no sense nor understanding of what it meant to be led by the "flesh." I realize now the reason was that I knew no truth, I had no comparison. Therein lies the reason why this chapter is so important.

I had a one-sided state of mind: the world centered around me, it was all about me; figuratively—kill or be killed. Luckily, I still had a conscience to act as a buffer sheltering me from overly pursuing my own selfishness and lawlessness. As I have come to learn, in the Christian world, it is defined as the battlefield of the mind.

If you have been a Christian for a while, you are acutely aware of our ever-present battlefield of the mind. As Apostle Paul put it in Romans 7:14-25:

The Conflict of Two Natures

> We know that the Law is spiritual, but I am a creature of the flesh [worldly, self-reliant—carnal and unspiritual], sold into slavery to sin [and serving under its control]. For I do not understand my own actions [I am baffled and bewildered by them]. I do not practice what I want to do, but I am doing the very thing I hate [and yielding to my human nature, my worldliness—my sinful capacity]. Now if I habitually do what I do not want to do, [that means] I agree with the Law, confessing that it is good (morally excellent). So now [if that is the case, then] it is no longer I who do it [the disobedient thing which I despise], but the sin [nature] which lives in me. For I know that nothing good lives in me, that is, in my flesh [my human nature, my worldliness—my sinful capacity]. For the willingness [to do good] is present in me, but the doing of good is not. For the good that I want to do, I do

> not do, but I practice the very evil that I do not want. But if I am doing the very thing I do not want to do, I am no longer the one doing it [that is, it is not me that acts], but the sin [nature] which lives in me.
>
> So I find it to be the law [of my inner self], that evil is present in me, the one who wants to do good. For I joyfully delight in the law of God in my inner self [with my new nature], but I see a different law and rule of action in the members of my body [in its appetites and desires], waging war against the law of my mind and subduing me and making me a prisoner of the law of sin which is within my members. Wretched and miserable man that I am! Who will [rescue me and] set me free from this body of death [this corrupt, mortal existence]? Thanks be to God [for my deliverance] through Jesus Christ our Lord! So then, on the one hand I myself with my mind serve the law of God, but on the other, with my flesh [my human nature, my worldliness, my sinful capacity—I serve] the law of sin.
>
> Romans 7:14-25 (AMP)

The battlefield of the mind has been written about quite extensively. One book comes to mind by Joyce Meyer, titled *Battlefield of the Mind*. If you have not read it yet, it is awesome. In her book, she details all the mental conflicts we suffer as Christians.

Literal Account of Romans 7:14-25

The literal account here is plainly seen: unbelievers acting only on their conscience, and Christians in a relationship with God, Jesus, and the Holy Spirit want to do good, but for the most part, do the opposite. It ends up being a vicious cycle producing much stress and anxiety. It is this very torment that kills us from the inside by wearing down the immune system.

Symbolic Account of Romans 7:14-25

Symbolically, this passage depicts the nature of God vs. the nature of the flesh. Going back to the second foundational truth stated in "Biblical Foundations," it is in our nature to rebel, causing us to be unkind and do evil. I want to expand on what I said in that section. I stated that the Trinity (God, Jesus, and the Holy Spirit) is the only force within the universe that represents *love*. Not human love, God's kind of *love* (agape)—supernatural *Love*. A description of God's kind of Love is found in 1 Corinthians 13.

The Excellence of Love

> Love endures with patience and serenity, love is kind and thoughtful, and is not jealous or envious; love does not brag and is not proud or arrogant. It is not rude; it is not self-seeking, it is not provoked [nor overly sensitive and easily angered]; it does not take into account a wrong endured. It does not rejoice at injustice, but rejoices with the truth [when right and truth prevail]. Love bears all things [regardless of what comes], believes all things [looking for the best in each one], hopes all things [remaining steadfast during difficult times], endures all things [without weakening]. Love never fails [it never fades nor ends].
>
> 1 Corinthians 13:4-8 (AMP)

Key point: if we are honest with ourselves, we must admit...we do not love like this. Why is that so important? I think it is imperative to point out that ultimately it is all about going to heaven or hell! Both places are eternal, and as such it puts God in the position of having to decide who goes and who does not. There was already one bad apple in heaven, and look at how much pain, suffering, and death that has created.

The Bible clearly states that the way God determines a person's worth is by the sincerity of their heart. What better way to determine what truly is in a person's heart than to test them under fire? I think most people would agree life is one big testing ground! With all that we experience in life, there is more than ample opportunity to prove one's sincerity.

Chapter Summary

Being double-minded drains our body's resources! It effectively generates a constant state of anxiety and stress. Long-term exposure to anxiety and stress has been medically proven to be the *greatest* detriment to our mental and physical health. In my second book, *Biblical Nutrition*, I will be showing you an extensive physiological comparison between the world's philosophy of how to be healthy and God's method.

In the next chapter, we will take an in-depth look at the mental and physical damages caused by trying to keep God's law.

Chapter Four

The Negative Neurological and Physiological Effects of Trying to Keep the Law

"Now just wait a minute...Red flag! Are you trying to tell me that keeping the Ten Commandments is killing me?" This is quite the paradox—yes, I am! "But I thought the commandments were holy" (they are) "and a guide to live by" (you could not keep them no matter how much will power you have).

Not to worry, here is the Biblical account:

> What shall we say then? Is the Law sin? Certainly not! On the contrary, if it had not been for the Law, I would not have recognized sin. For I would not have known [for example] about coveting [what belongs to another, and would have had no sense of guilt] if the Law had not [repeatedly] said, "YOU SHALL NOT COVET." But sin, finding an opportunity through the commandment [to express itself] produced in me every kind of coveting and selfish desire. For without the Law sin is dead [the recognition of sin is inactive]. I was once alive without [knowledge of] the Law; but when the commandment came [and I understood its meaning], sin became alive and I died [since the Law sentenced me to death]. And the very commandment, which was intended to bring life, actually proved to bring death for me. For sin, seizing its opportunity through the commandment, beguiled and completely deceived me, and using it as a weapon killed me [separating me from God]. So then, the Law is holy, and the commandment is holy and righteous and good.
>
> Did that which is good [the Law], then become death to me? Certainly not! But sin, in order that it might be revealed as sin, was producing death in me by [using] this good thing [as a weapon], so that through the commandment sin would become exceedingly sinful.
>
> Romans 7:7-13 (AMP)

The second fresh new revelation

First and foremost, the Ten Commandments were not given to all people as we have been led to believe. If you know the Biblical account, Moses came down from Mount Sinai (in the middle of the desert), and the only people there were the Jews. It was a covenant between God and the Jews only!

> (Indeed, when Gentiles, who do not have the law, do by nature things required by the law, they are a law for themselves, even though they do not have the law.
>
> Romans 2:14 (NIV)

Okay, you got me there, but what about the Ten Commandments being holy and a guide to live by? Well, let us see what the Bible says:

The Greater Glory of the New Covenant

> Now if the ministry that brought death, which was engraved in letters on stone, came with glory, so that the Israelites could not look steadily at the face of Moses because of its glory, transitory though it was, will not the ministry of the Spirit be even more glorious? If the ministry that brought condemnation was glorious, how much more glorious is the ministry that brings righteousness! For what was glorious has no glory now in comparison with the surpassing glory. And if what was transitory came with glory, how much greater is the glory of that which lasts!
>
> Therefore, since we have such a hope, we are very bold. We are not like Moses, who would put a veil over his face to prevent the Israelites from seeing the end of what was passing away. But their minds were made dull, for to this day the same veil remains when the old covenant is read. It has not been removed, because only in Christ is it taken away. Even to this day when Moses is read, a veil covers their hearts. But whenever anyone turns to the Lord, the veil is taken away. Now the Lord is the Spirit, and where the Spirit

> of the Lord is, there is freedom. And we all, who with unveiled faces contemplate the Lord's glory, are being transformed into his image with ever-increasing glory, which comes from the Lord, who is the Spirit.
>
> 2 Corinthians 3:7-18 (NIV)

The Literal Account of 2 Corinthians 3:7-18

- Starting with verse 7, there is only one ministry in history that was engraved on two physical pieces of stone, the Ten Commandments (physical laws). This verse also clearly states that this ministry brought physical death! According to the Bible, Jesus was not put to death because He broke a Roman law; He was put to death because He broke Jewish law (Ten Commandments) by committing blasphemy. Verse 7 also clearly states that the Ten Commandants came with "glory" (they are Holy). Do not panic here, it will all come clear as you read further. According to the Biblical account of the day God gave the Ten Commandments to the Jews, 3,000 people died.

Moses turned and went down the mountain with the two tablets of the covenant law in his hands. They were inscribed on both sides, front and back. The tablets were the work of God; the writing was the writing of God, engraved on the tablets.

When Joshua heard the noise of the people shouting, he said to Moses, "There is the sound of war in the camp."

Moses replied:

"It is not the sound of victory,
  it is not the sound of defeat;
  it is the sound of singing that I hear."
When Moses approached the camp and saw the calf and the dancing, his anger burned and he threw the tablets out of his hands, breaking

them to pieces at the foot of the mountain. And he took the calf the people had made and burned it in the fire; then he ground it to powder, scattered it on the water and made the Israelites drink it.

He said to Aaron, "What did these people do to you, that you led them into such great sin?"

"Do not be angry, my lord," Aaron answered. "You know how prone these people are to evil. [23] They said to me, 'Make us gods who will go before us. As for this fellow Moses who brought us up out of Egypt, we don't know what has happened to him.' So I told them, 'Whoever has any gold jewelry, take it off.' Then they gave me the gold, and I threw it into the fire, and out came this calf!"

Moses saw that the people were running wild and that Aaron had let them get out of control and so become a laughingstock to their enemies. So he stood at the entrance to the camp and said, "Whoever is for the LORD, come to me." And all the Levites rallied to him.

Then he said to them, "This is what the LORD, the God of Israel, says: 'Each man strap a sword to his side. Go back and forth through the camp from one end to the other, each killing his brother and friend and neighbor.'" The Levites did as Moses commanded, and that day about three thousand of the people died.

Exodus 32:15-28 (NIV)

- 2 Corinthians 3, Verse 9 goes on to state the Ten Commandments brought condemnation. Not only does being under condemnation not feel good, physiologically, it produces very high levels of fear, stress, and anxiety.
- Verses 14-16 tell us that whenever the old covenant is read (the Ten Commandments), it creates a literal veil (the physical item of separation) between us and God. If you remember, I pointed this out in Chapter 1. Knowing the

difference between good vs. evil is what created the physical separation between man and God (the veil). The physical nature of this veil covers/covered the hearts of the Jews. The only force in the universe which can remove the veil is the person Jesus Christ.

- Verses 17-18 brings us back to the GOoD news! Any person who accepts (confesses with their mouth and believes in their heart) Jesus as their personal Savior receives the Spirit of the Lord, producing freedom (release from fear, stress, and anxiety). Accepting Jesus removes the veil, brings us back into the relationship with the Trinity, and begins the transformation process.

The Symbolic Account of 2 Corinthians 3:7-18

All these verses are defining the spiritual difference between the Old Covenant follower and the New Covenant follower.

If you remember from Chapter 1, adopting (eating the fruit), buying into the state of mind defined in the Bible as "The Law" (following the Ten Commandments) is what spiritually separated us from God (veiled). Semantically, do good—get good! Do bad—get bad! Anything and everything that has to do with trying to earn salvation through our own efforts is considered works of the flesh and brings only death. Biblically, this state of mind is referred to as the Law of sin and death (our sinful nature).

Spiritually, any person who is trying to live by the Law will have a dull mind, and their heart will be hardened (full of resentfulness and anger).

Pretty gruesome...but not to worry, here is the Biblical GOoD news to offset the gruesomeness.

> At that moment the curtain of the temple was torn in two from top to bottom. The earth shook, the rocks split.
>
> Matthew 27:51 (NIV)

And Peter said to them, "Repent [change your old way of thinking, turn from your sinful ways, accept and follow Jesus as the Messiah] and be baptized, each of you, in the name of Jesus Christ because of the forgiveness of your sins; and you will receive the gift of the Holy Spirit. For the promise [of the Holy Spirit] is for you and your children and for all who are far away [including the Gentiles], as many as the Lord our God calls to Himself." And Peter solemnly testified and continued to admonish and urge them with many more words, saying, "Be saved from this crooked and unjust generation!" So then, those who accepted his message were baptized; and on that day about 3,000 souls were added [to the body of believers]. They were continually and faithfully devoting themselves to the instruction of the apostles, and to fellowship, to eating meals together and to prayers.

Acts 2:38-42 (AMP)

So also we [whether Jews or Gentiles], when we were children (spiritually immature), were kept like slaves under the elementary [man-made religious or philosophical] teachings of the world. But when [in God's plan] the proper time had fully come, God sent His Son, born of a woman, born under the [regulations of the] Law, so that He might redeem and liberate those who were under the Law, that we [who believe] might be adopted as sons [as God's children with all rights as fully grown members of a family]. And because you [really] are [His] sons, God has sent the Spirit of His Son into our hearts, crying out, "Abba! Father!" Therefore you are no longer a slave (bond-servant), but a son; and if a son, then also an heir through [the gracious act of] God [through Christ].

Galatians 4:3-7 (AMP)

Whoever believes and has decided to trust in Him [as personal Savior and Lord] is not judged [for this one, there is no judgment, no rejection, no condemnation]; but the one who does not believe [and has decided to reject Him as personal Savior and Lord] is judged already [that one has been convicted and sentenced],

> because he has not believed and trusted in the name of the [One and] only begotten Son of God [the One who is truly unique, the only One of His kind, the One who alone can save him].
>
> John 3:18 (AMP)

Key point: Comparing Exodus 32:15-28 (Old Testament) and Acts 2:38-42 (New Testament) exemplifies the contrast between the Old Testament and the New Testament. The Old Testament was all about man wanting tangible ways to earn salvation. Man wanted laws, kings, and idols to worship. None of which produced salvation, only death (physically and spiritually). Conversely, the New Testament is all about what Jesus did for us! It is all about His grace and mercy leading us to salvation and a healthy life.

The third fresh new revelation

2 Corinthians 3:7-18 makes it exceedingly clear the Old Testament has faded away, and according to God, we are now under the New Testament. Strangely, even though the Bible makes it abundantly clear, there are still churches today that are preaching Old Testament ministry. Whether the Pastors/Priests know it or not, they are veiling the congregation and separating them from the very thing they are going to church for, to learn about Jesus and how He uses grace to set us free from the condemnation of the law. Ironically, this veiling (law mindset) nullifies the power of Jesus to change us through His Grace. Again, not to worry—Jesus has set us free. Here is the Bible account:

> Therefore there is now no condemnation [no guilty verdict, no punishment] for those who are in Christ Jesus [who believe in Him as personal Lord and Savior]. For the law of the Spirit of life [which is] in Christ Jesus [the law of our new being] has set you free from the law of sin and of death. For what the Law could not do [that is, overcome sin and remove its penalty, its power] being weakened by the flesh [man's nature without the Holy Spirit], God did: He sent His own Son in the likeness of sinful man as

> an offering for sin. And He condemned sin in the flesh [subdued it and overcame it in the person of His own Son], so that the [righteous and just] requirement of the Law might be fulfilled in us who do not live our lives in the ways of the flesh [guided by worldliness and our sinful nature], but [live our lives] in the ways of the Spirit [guided by His power].
>
> Romans 8:1-4 (AMP)

Clarification point: I am not saying the Old Testament should not be read and is not for believers even though it has passed away. The New Testament is the fulfillment of the Old Testament. The Old Testament, with its laws defining good and evil, is necessary to understand the New Testament's fulfillment purpose of Jesus' death and resurrection to bring us salvation with grace and mercy, and His ultimate reconciliation to mankind.

> know that a person is not justified by the works of the law, but by faith in Jesus Christ. So we, too, have put our faith in Christ Jesus that we may be justified by faith in[a] Christ and not by the works of the law, because by the works of the law no one will be justified.
>
> Galatians 2:16 (NIV)

Let me simplify this a little further: a testament is a contract like your car loan agreement. You signed a testament (contract) to make payments monthly for your car. Let's say your testament agreed to 60 payments. You are now at month 61: your car loan has been paid in full.

It does not make any sense, nor are you obligated to make a payment on the 61st month, as it is paid in full! Clarification point: at no point am I suggesting that a believer should continue to live in sin.

Here is the Biblical account.

> What then [are we to conclude]? Shall we sin because we are not under Law, but under [God's] grace? Certainly not! Do you not

> know that when you continually offer yourselves to someone to do his will, you are the slaves of the one whom you obey, either [slaves] of sin, which leads to death, or of obedience, which leads to righteousness (right standing with God)? But thank God that though you were slaves of sin, you became obedient with all your heart to the standard of teaching in which you were instructed and to which you were committed. And having been set free from sin, you have become the slaves of righteousness [of conformity to God's will and purpose]. I am speaking in [familiar] human terms because of your natural limitations [your spiritual immaturity]. For just as you presented your bodily members as slaves to impurity and to [moral] lawlessness, leading to further lawlessness, so now offer your members [your abilities, your talents] as slaves to righteousness, leading to sanctification [that is, being set apart for God's purpose].
>
> Romans 6:15-19 (AMP)

The Old Testament was based on self-effort, the ability to keep the Ten Commandments in addition to all of the Levitical Laws (in total, 613). The payment for not keeping just one of these laws was death. Conversely, the New Testament is based on Grace and not self-effort. Jesus paid, in full, for everyone's sin with His death on the cross.

> Consequently, just as one trespass resulted in condemnation for all people, so also one righteous act resulted in justification and life for all people. For just as through the disobedience of the one man the many were made sinners, so also through the obedience of the one man the many will be made righteous.
>
> Romans 5:18-19 (NIV)

The New Testament has only two commandments given to us by Jesus.

> Jesus replied: "'Love the Lord your God with all your heart and with all your soul and with all your mind. This is the first and

> greatest commandment. And the second is like it: 'Love your neighbor as yourself. '
>
> Matthew 22:37-39 (NIV)

> Owe nothing to anyone except to love and seek the best for one another; for he who [unselfishly] loves his neighbor has fulfilled the [essence of the] law [relating to one's fellowman]. The commandments, "You shall not commit adultery, you shall not murder, you shall not steal, you shall not covet," and any other commandment are summed up in this statement: "You shall love your neighbor as yourself." Love does no wrong to a neighbor [it never hurts anyone]. Therefore [unselfish] love is the fulfillment of the Law.

> Do this, knowing that this is a critical time. It is already the hour for you to awaken from your sleep [of spiritual complacency]; for our salvation is nearer to us now than when we first believed [in Christ]. The night [this present evil age] is almost gone and the day [of Christ's return] is almost here. So let us fling away the works of darkness and put on the [full] armor of light. Let us conduct ourselves properly and honorably as in the [light of] day, not in carousing and drunkenness, not in sexual promiscuity and irresponsibility, not in quarreling and jealousy. But clothe yourselves with the Lord Jesus Christ, and make no provision for [nor even think about gratifying] the flesh in regard to its improper desires.
>
> Romans 13:8-14 (AMP)

Chapter Summary

The summary for this chapter is the same as that of Chapter 3 with one difference. The negative physiological driving force this time is condemnation. In my second book, *Biblical Nutrition*, I will be showing you how condemnation increases stress and anxiety, which alters our nutritional intake making it very difficult to be emotionally stable.

Chapter Five

Sticks and Stones May Break My Bones, but Words Can Never Harm Me

Wow, wow, wow...quite possibly the greatest lie we tell our children! Apparently, this phrase originally appeared in a publication called *The Christian Recorder* back in 1892. It was created as a response to an insult, implying that "You might be able to hurt me by physical force but not by insults." It rapidly became a stock response to verbal bullying, most often used on playgrounds across the English-speaking world.

As you will learn later in this chapter, words are not only the triggers of every action we take, but they also ultimately control our *destiny*. In Chapter 6, I will provide you with Biblical and scientific proof that words are energy, and as such, they are giving substance to and are creating our world. If you are not sure they are that powerful, consider this.

Is it not true...if you tell a three, four, or five-year-old they are stupid, lazy, and good for nothing, what happens? Correct, for the most part, that is exactly what they will become. While not all children become it, sadly, the math is above the 90% level. This has been going on for thousands and thousands of years.

Foundationally, this is the *most* important part of this book! Let me break this down further. A three, four, or five-year-old is a blank slate at that point in their life. Surely, they are not stupid, lazy, and good for nothing. Yes, maybe they did something to cause the wrath of their parent(s), but if the parent(s) continue to speak those words into the child's life, it effectively forces the child into a corner where they must make a decision.

Do I believe my parent(s) or not? Technically, it does not matter whether a person is a child or an adult. Insults occur, in one form or another, throughout all our lives. Ultimately forcing us to decide.

Key point: there is a variable involved, though, that controls the child's or adult's destiny. Would you venture to take a guess what controls whether or not the person becomes what they are being told? It is their belief!

Going back to the example: even though he/she is young and effectively a blank slate, if they end up believing in their heart (the heart has neurons just like the ones in our brain) they are stupid, lazy, and good for nothing, as they grow older is when they become it! *They are not it initially, they are a blank slate!* The words controlled their *destiny!* Be sure to meditate on the summary at the end of the chapter.

In addition to the Word of God, there are many other words we experience in our life. There are the words spoken to us by other people, positive or negative; there are the words we speak to ourselves in our mind, positive or negative, and believers know the devil speaks to us through thoughts, ideas, and suggestions. It surely was not God who told the man to pick up a gun, go into the mall and start shooting people—that guy was listening to the wrong voice.

Please bear with me here. Words are the *core theme* of this book and the building blocks, affecting the changes we all need to make in our lives. Let us look at what the Bible says about the tongue. Biblical facts: the word tongue appears 126 times in the Bible and is found in 34 books. Here are just a few accounts.

> From the fruit of their mouth a person's stomach is filled; with the harvest of their lips they are satisfied. The tongue has the power of life and death, and those who love it will eat its fruit.
>
> Proverbs 18:20-21(NIV)

There is that phrase again..."eat of its fruit!" Hopefully, you remembered from Chapter 2 that eating of fruit symbolically means to buy into that way of thinking. If we believe in the words being spoken to us, or even worst, the negative words we are saying in our mind to ourselves, we will become it. Here are more Biblical accounts.

Now if we put bits into the horses' mouths to make them obey us, we guide their whole body as well. And look at the ships. Even though they are so large and are driven by strong winds, they are still directed by a very small rudder wherever the impulse of the helmsman determines. In the same sense, the tongue is a small part of the body, and yet it boasts of great things.

See [by comparison] how great a forest is set on fire by a small spark! And the tongue is [in a sense] a fire, the very world of injustice and unrighteousness; the tongue is set among our members as that which contaminates the entire body, and sets on fire the course of our life [the cycle of man's existence], and is itself set on fire by hell (Gehenna).

James 3:3-6 (AMP)

Those who guard their mouths and their tongues keep themselves from calamity.

Proverbs 21:23 (NIV)

A gentle answer turns away wrath, but a harsh word stir up anger.

Proverbs 15:1 (NIV)

With their mouths the godless destroy their neighbors; but through knowledge the righteous escape.

Proverbs 11:9 (NIV)

Evildoers are trapped by their sinful talk, and so the innocent escape trouble. From the fruit of their lips people are filled with good things, and the work of their hands brings them reward."

Proverbs 12:13-14(NIV)

Let us go deeper still!

It blew me away when the Holy Spirit unpacked the depth of words we hear from the world (media). The Holy Spirit asked me, "if you walk up and down the street and ask people, 'do you think the world is falling apart?' what do you think most people would say"?

Yep, most would say, definitely...*wrong!*

Here is the math, according to Wikipedia:

> At the end of 2016, the Prison Policy Initiative, a non-profit organization for decarceration, estimated that in the United States, about 2,298,300 people were incarcerated out of a population of 324.2 million. This means that 0.7% of the population was behind bars. Of those who were incarcerated, about 1,316,000 people were in state prison, 615,000 in local jails, 225,000 in federal prisons, 48,000 in youth correctional facilities, 34,000 in immigration detention camps, 22,000 in involuntary commitment, 11,000 in territorial prisons, 2,500 in Indian Country jails, and 1,300 in the United States military prisons.[2]

Again....*Wow, wow, and wow*! Mathematically, less than 1% of the population of the United States are criminals, yet our perception is the world is falling apart. How is this possible? Have you ever thought about how much stress and anxiety this causes? Who altered our perception? *The media*!

Everyone knows bad news sells, but have you ever really thought about the consequences of only hearing bad news? Exactly, it has effectively altered our perception of life. Sadly, the bad-news-sells concept is found in all forms of media, print, radio, TV, and social media. The net result of hundreds of years of bad news is a subliminal mindset of constant fear and worry.

Here is one more example to cement this in your mind. I live in the Atlanta, Georgia, area, which has a population of 498,044 (2016). Example: I watched the news (I do not watch the news anymore) last night, and there were five people shot. Doing the math...dividing 5 by 498,044 = 1% of the population, yet subliminally we conclude Atlanta must be a dangerous place. Crazy, right!

So how do words alter our perception? The word diagram below is a great illustration of how words control our life.

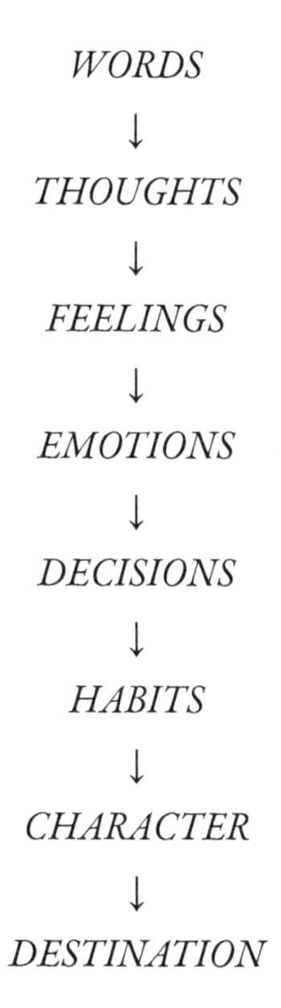

The Holy Spirit confirmed the magnitude of words to me in an interview I watched on Trinity Broadcast Network (TBN) with Dr. Creflo Dollar. This simple diagram illustrates how words affect our thoughts, our thoughts guide our feelings, our feelings shape our emotions, our emotions absolutely control our decisions in life, our decisions in life create our habits, our habits in life define our character, and our character controls our destination in life.

As incredible as that is, it is even more powerful when you go backward. If a person is not happy with their destination in life (where they are at today), what does that person have to do to change their destination? Go in reverse order! They have to change their character, but a person cannot change their character until they change their habits, they cannot change their habits until they make better decisions and continuing up the ladder...it goes right back to words.

Key point: Studying God's Word is what changes us by renewing our minds! Going deeper still, God guarantees that if you follow His Word, you and your family will be saved and will have the best possible destination in life.

> "I assure you and most solemnly say to you, the person who hears My word [the one who heeds My message], and believes and trusts in Him who sent Me, has (possesses now) eternal life [that is, eternal life actually begins—the believer is transformed], and does not come into judgment and condemnation, but has passed [over] from death into life.
>
> John 5:24 (AMP)

> They replied, "Believe in the Lord Jesus, and you will be saved—you and your household."
>
> Acts 16:31 (NIV)

> The thief comes only to steal and kill and destroy; I have come that they may have life, and have it to the full.
>
> John 10:10 (NIV)

Chapter Summary

Connecting the dots, think about it: if you do not get your words from the Bible, where do you get your words from? *Your environment (the people who surround you) and the media!*

If a person allows the words generated by the environment/media to dictate their thoughts, feelings, emotions, decisions, habits, and character, they will have the worst possible destination in life. You can think about it this way: imagine what your life would be like if you could afford to live like this.

You wake up in the morning, turn on the news, and watch the news all day until you go to bed for one full year. You would be neurotic! You wouldn't be able to sleep at night because of fear your home might be broken into, you wouldn't want to go outside because you might get mugged, you wouldn't want to drive your car because it might get carjacked, and you wouldn't want to go shopping in a mall because some nut with a gun might be there and shoot you.

Basically, you would have no hope! Exactly what the devil wants.

Chapter Six

Quantum Words of Faith

What I am about to share with you is the bonding agent that ensures you will overcome all of the hurdles on your journey to lasting change—*faith*! As I mentioned, my complete recovery took ten years, of which the first three were absolutely brutal. The glue that held it all together was my faith that God would do what He promised: take the worst day of my life and turn it into the best day of my life.

So, let us start out with what God says about His commitment to helping us move through every hurdle. Here is the Biblical account:

> Let your character [your moral essence, your inner nature] be free from the love of money [shun greed—be financially ethical], being content with what you have; for He has said, "I will never [under any circumstances] desert you [nor give you up nor leave you without support, nor will I in any degree leave you helpless], nor will I forsake or let you down or relax My hold on you [assuredly not]!"
>
> Hebrews 13:5 (AMP)

Because you are reading this book, you will have a distinct advantage I did not have. Your advantage is the scientific evidence that proves everything God said to do by faith does change us from the inside out.

The following is quoted from the book *Quantum Faith* by Annette Capps (which I highly recommend reading—I have read it more than 50 times in the past 15 years, it is that amazing).

Before we look at the Biblical definition of faith, I want to share another *major* Biblical principle with you. Quantum Faith, page 11: "*things obey words!*" Biblical proof coming right up!

Now on one of those days Jesus and His disciples got into a boat, and He said to them, "Let us cross over to the other side of the lake (Sea of Galilee)." So they set out. But as they were sailing, He fell asleep. And a fierce gale of wind swept down [as if through a wind tunnel] on the lake, and they began to be swamped, and were in great danger. They came to Jesus and woke Him, saying, "Master, Master, we are about to die!" He got up and rebuked the wind and the raging, violent waves, and they ceased, and it became calm [a perfect peacefulness]. And He said to them, "Where is your faith [your confidence in Me]?" They were afraid and astonished, saying to one another, "Who then is this, that He commands even the winds and the sea, and they obey Him?"

Luke 8:22-25 (AMP)

And the Lord said, "If you have [confident, abiding] faith in God [even as small] as a mustard seed, you could say to this mulberry tree [which has very strong roots], 'Be pulled up by the roots and be planted in the sea'; and [if the request was in agreement with the will of God] it would have obeyed you.

Luke 17:6 (AMP)

Jesus replied, "Have faith in God [constantly]. I assure you and most solemnly say to you, whoever says to this mountain, 'Be lifted up and thrown into the sea!' and does not doubt in his heart [in God's unlimited power], but believes that what he says is going to take place, it will be done for him [in accordance with God's will]. For this reason I am telling you, whatever things you ask for in prayer [in accordance with God's will], believe [with confident trust] that you have received them, and they will be given to you. Whenever you stand praying, if you have anything against anyone, forgive him [drop the issue, let it go], so that your Father who is in heaven will also forgive you your transgressions and wrongdoings [against Him and others].

Mark 11:22-25 (AMP)

Key point by Quantum Faith:

> He spoke to the wind and the waves, they obeyed Him. Jesus did not demonstrate this Biblical principle just to prove He was the Son of God. He demonstrated it and then told His disciple that they too can speak words of power. He wanted us to have the revelation that we are powerful Spiritual beings who can speak to the mountains in our life and they will obey us.[3]

> I love those verses! Now here is what the Bible has to say about faith.

> Now faith is the assurance (title deed, confirmation) of things hoped for (divinely guaranteed), and the evidence of things not seen [the conviction of their reality—faith comprehends as fact what cannot be experienced by the physical senses]. For by this [kind of] faith the men of old gained [divine] approval. By faith [that is, with an inherent trust and enduring confidence in the power, wisdom and goodness of God] we understand that the worlds (universe, ages) were framed and created [formed, put in order, and equipped for their intended purpose] by the word of God, so that what is seen was not made out of things which are visible.
>
> Hebrews 11:1-3 (AMP)

From a literal standpoint, these verses raise quite a few questions. How can there be evidence of something we cannot see? How can we comprehend what we cannot touch, taste, see, smell, and hear? How can something be created with something we cannot see?

So why is the title of this chapter "Quantum Words of Faith"? "What in the world does quantum physics have to do with words and faith?" I am so glad you asked that question!

Quantum Faith reads, "Quantum Physics is the study of things so small we cannot see them, yet everything we see is made up of these subatomic particles." A perfect example of the principle of faith in Hebrews 11:3 "so that what is seen was not made out of thing which are visible" is water (H2O). "Before the hydrogen and oxygen combined into water, you could not see anything, yet the substance for water was there."[4]

Let's go back to Luke 17:6 because it is the perfect lead-in to what quantum physics has to do with words and faith. Jesus said, "if you have the faith of a mustard seed," you could say, "Jesus was speaking of the smallest seed that could be seen in His time."

> If He were here today, He might say "if had the faith of an atom..." Or even smaller, "if you had the faith as a quark (which is a subatomic particle)..." The point He was making was that small things that cannot be easily seen can manifest themselves and affect things in this larger world where we live.[5]

The fourth fresh new revelation

Most unbelievers (and even some long-time believers) who read the following verse think Jesus was being ridiculous and speaking only figuratively...or maybe He was downright crazy!

> I assure you and most solemnly say to you, whoever says to this mountain, "Be lifted up and thrown into the sea!" and does not doubt in his heart [in God's unlimited power], but believes that what he says is going to take place, it will be done for him [in accordance with God's will].
>
> Mark 11:23 (AMP)

It is only by faith a person believes that you *can* have what you say! How can words be that powerful? The science of quantum physics proves that what Jesus said in Mark 11:23 is an absolute scientific fact! Our words are creating the substance of our world (where we are at in life).

Think of it this way: spoken words send out sound vibrations. Quantum physics has proven that the sound vibration of spoken words is an energy, and energy affects matter.

And God said, "Let there be light"; and there was light.

Genesis 1:3 (NIV)

The substance of light was there; it just needed His Word vibrations to make it manifest. Here are a few examples of how energy affects matter. *Quantum Faith*:

> The energy of your microwave vibrates the water molecules and heats the water. The energy of electricity flows to your washing machine and powers the motor that spins the tub and cleans your clothes. Your words are energy, and they affect the matter in your life! When you speak the words, "This is the worst car I have ever had! You stupid piece of junk!" Those words are vibrations of energy that affect the atoms that make up that car. If you speak those words long enough, your car will obey you![6]

Key point: Quantum Faith, page 9: "the substance from which our world is made is influenced and manifested by words and our beliefs. The things you desire are made up of atoms. They know what you believe, hear what you say, and behave accordingly!"

Additionally, *Quantum Faith* says:

> The thoughts and beliefs that you carry also produce an energy around you. Have you ever noticed that when you are angry, things go wrong, and people are insulting and angry with you? Your thoughts and beliefs produce an energy that people can perceive and react to.
>
> If you believe no one likes you, you emit that rejecting type of energy, and people will be driven away from you. Conversely, if you love people and care about them, they will feel that and be drawn to you. Have you ever been around someone who is pleasant and full of love? It is an energy you can feel. The energy of love is a powerful drawing card for good in your life. After all, God is Love.[7]

Key point: Quantum Faith, page 10: "God is not limited to the things you and I see. There is an infinite supply of substance just waiting to be manifested according to your beliefs and words!"

Breaking it down even more, Quantum Faith specifies:

All "things" (matter) are made of atoms, including your children, car, computer, and your house. None of these "things" is solid, including your kitchen table even if it is made of oak. You may not be able to see the space between the atoms in your table, but if you could see that small, you would also see movement. That's right! Your kitchen table is vibrating! Everything has a frequency of vibration. We vibrate, our car vibrates, and even the mountain behind your house vibrates. They all have a nature frequency.

...to our example of the microwave heating your cup of water. How does it do that? The frequency vibration of microwaves is much higher than that of water. When those high frequency waves begin to bombard the water molecules, the electrons in the atoms are excited and move more and more rapidly (a higher vibration). The result is that the substance (water) becomes hotter. The electrons have jumped to a higher orbit changing the behavior of your water into boiling. When we introduce cold temperature to water, it slows down the vibrations of the atomic structure to such a degree the water becomes more solid and freezes.[8]

Key point by Quantum Faith:

"All" things respond to the vibration of energy. That begs the question of what kind of energy are we producing? Do we want our water boiling or frozen? Are you introducing faith-energized high frequency words and beliefs to your children, finances, and health? Or do you introduce low frequency, negative words that freeze your circumstances into a continual series of crises and destroy our health"? [9]

Chapter Summary

As you have learned so far, these recent scientific discoveries have provided proof God's Word has been guiding mankind on a path guaranteed to produce change all a long. What is important here is that we can, with faithful confidence trust in God to do what He promises over and over in His Word to do – change us from the inside out. So, stay in faith and spend time with God by reading His Word continually! There simply is no substitute. In the next chapter we will learn how to know (discern) when you are hearing God speaking to us.

Chapter Seven

Achieving Discernment (Hearing God's voice) by Meditating on God's Word

Prayerfully, you are hanging in there with me. Like most of you, I was more of a McDonalds' kind of solution person. It is so hard to wait! Truly, truly I say to you: after struggling with, for some of you, boring neurological facts, when you get to the end of the chapter, your reward might just produce the *largest chill bumps* you have ever experienced.

Please be sure to read this chapter slowly and in a quiet place where you can meditate (deeply ponder) on what I am about to share. Hopefully, you remembered what I shared in Chapter 3 about our two natures: the flesh and the devil's agenda (stinking thinking). For it is the combination of these ways of thinking that need to be renewed to effectively hear God's Word, leading us to the freedom and the peace of mind He is offering us. Not only does stinking thinking lead to negative/hurtful attitudes/words, destructive aggression, hate, violence, and war, they destroy our health along the way.

Conversely, God's plan is to reverse our stinking thinking into His way of thinking. Learning the value of thinking in God's way and showing the science/physiology behind it is the main purpose of this book.

The fifth fresh new revelation

By the time you finish this book, you will clearly see the Beauty and Love of God's plan for redeeming us from our stinking thinking. For it is God's hope that one day the "man" we all carry within us might free himself from the animal that we also carry within us. God is the ultimate neurobiologist for sure, but how can we understand the process of "renewing our mind" if we are never informed about how this admirable mechanism called the nervous system works?

> And do not be conformed to this world [any longer with its superficial values and customs], but be transformed and progressively changed [as you mature spiritually] by the renewing of your mind [focusing on godly values and ethical attitudes], so that you may prove [for yourselves] what the will of God is, that which is good and acceptable and perfect [in His plan and purpose for you].
>
> Romans 12:2 (AMP)

First, let us look at what Wikipedia has to say about Christian discernment:

> Christian spiritual discernment can be separated from other types of discernment because every decision is to be made by following God's will. The fundamental definition of Christian discernment is a decision-making process in which an individual makes a discovery that can lead to future action. In the process of Christian spiritual discernment, God guides the individual to help them arrive at the best decision. The way to arrive at the best decision in Christian spiritual discernment is to seek out internal/external signs of God's action and then apply them to the decision at hand. Christian Discernment also has an emphasis on Jesus and making decisions that align with those of Jesus within the New Testament. The focus on God and Jesus when making decisions is what separates Christian discernment from secular discernment.[10]

Simplifying it, when I think about this word (discernment), a picture comes to my mind. I might be dating myself here, but back in the day, while watching cartoons (I think it was Elmer Fudd), there was a scene with him standing there pondering with an angel on one shoulder and the devil on the other shoulder. Both were whispering in his ear.

The sixth fresh new revelation

During my recovery period, while I was living in Fort Myers, Florida, the Holy Spirit directed me to a Christian church where I met Rev. Daryl Sanders. I attended his Bible study group for a couple of years. His pet saying was, "you cannot just read the Bible...you have to READ the Bible." At first, I was not sure what that actually meant. It took me a couple of months to figure it out.

It has everything to do with discernment, the hearing of God's voice. Let me break it down again for you. It is a decision-making process in which a person is listening to the conversation going on in their mind (generated by neuropathways) with the determination of identifying who is doing the talking. Again, an angel on one shoulder and a devil on the other. If you do not remember, in "Foundational Insights," I was talking about "not knowing what I did not know." Well, before my death, even though I had read the Bible from cover to cover three times from 20 to 50 years old, after meeting Pastor Sanders, I realized what I was doing was just reading the Bible.

I did not *READ* it with Spiritual eyes looking for the mysteries hidden within directed by the Holy Spirit. So effectively, I knew who God was, but I had no relationship with Him. The reason being was because I had no discernment. I had no ability to recognize His voice as opposed to the flesh/devil's voice, i.e., I had nothing to compare it to.

Key point: the purpose of this book is to share the science/physiology behind how God changes us from the inside out. The problem is, without the foundational information provided in this book, it will not make sense. So, let us talk about some foundational neurobiology.

Understanding where the positive/negative words (the foundation of discernment) that we speak to ourselves in our mind come from requires a comprehension of how they are created neurologically. Remember the word diagram—words control our thoughts! Example:

if I were to say to you that you are a very bad person, it would instantly trigger a unique conversation (voice) within your mind that effectively is a summation of all of the negative things stored in your memory.

Conversely, if I said to you, you are a very good person, it would instantly trigger a unique conversation (voice) within your mind that effectively is a summation of all of the positive things stored in your memory.

Neurology 101

So, to understand where the words come from, we need to understand what a neuron is and its associated pathway. When you think of a neuropathway, imagine a tree!

A healthy neuropathway indeed looks like a tree with a full canopy. There is a trunk, which is the cell's nucleus; there is a root system, embodied in a single axon; and there are the branches, called dendrites.

Neurons in your brain pass signals from one to another like they are playing an elaborate, lightning-quick game of telephone, using axons as the transmitters and dendrites as the receivers. Those signals originate in the brain and are passed throughout the body, culminating in simple actions, such as wiggling a toe, to more complex instructions, such as following through on a thought.

According to brainfacts.org,

> neurons are cells within the nervous system that capture data and transmit their information to other nerve cells, muscle, or gland cells. Most neurons have a cell body, an axon, and dendrites. The cell body contains the nucleus and cytoplasm. The axon extends from the cell body and often gives rise to many smaller branches before ending at nerve terminals. Dendrites extend from the neuron cell body and receive messages from other neurons. Synapses are the contact points where one neuron communicates with another. The dendrites are covered with synapses formed by the ends of axons from other neurons.[11]

According to Scientific America,

> the question of just how much information our brains can hold is a longstanding one. We know that the human brain is made up of about 100 billion neurons and that each one makes 1,000 or more connections to other neurons, adding up to some 100 trillion in total. We also know that the strengths of these connections, or synapses, are regulated by experience.[12]

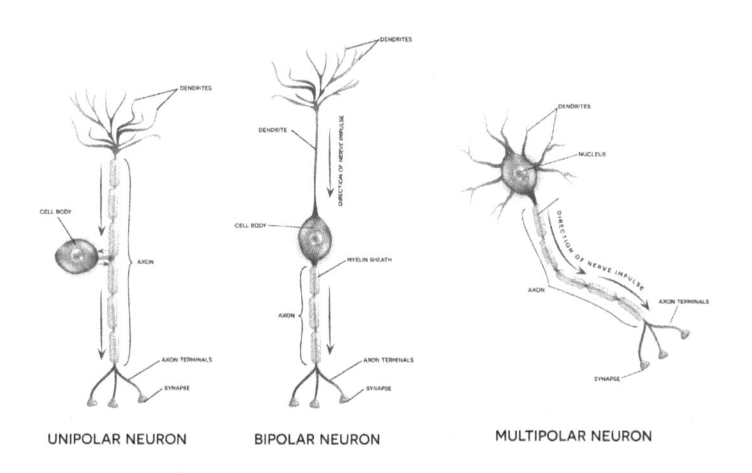

According to The Brain from Top to Bottom,

> every time you learn something, neural circuits are altered in your brain. These circuits are composed of several neurons (nerve cells) that communicate with one another through special junctions called synapses.
>
> When you learn something, it is these synapses whose efficiency increases, thus facilitating the passage of nerve impulses along a particular circuit. For example, when you are exposed to a new word, you have to make new connections among certain neurons

in your brain to deal with it: some neurons in your visual cortex to recognize the spelling, others in your auditory cortex to hear the pronunciation, and still others in the associative regions of the cortex to relate the word to your existing knowledge.

To learn this new word, you repeat it to yourself several times, and this selects and strengthens the connections among these various circuits in your cortex. And it is this new, durable association among certain neurons that will form your memory of this word. The strength of this association may of course depend on several factors.[13]

Specifically, how many times it is reinforced.

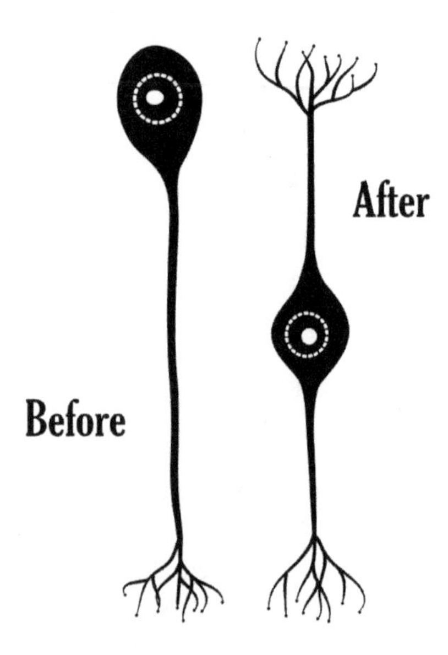

Key point: the before picture illustrates a neuron without a pathway, and the after picture illustrates a complete neuropathway. As we learned above, repetition, which really is meditation, changes a neuron into a neuropathway. This is a critical point because (as I will demonstrate later in this chapter) completed neuropathways generate words!

Understanding the Synapse

To complete our understanding of neurobiology, we need to take a closer look at the synapse. Recapping, neurons store information by a process called meditation. The meditation process causes the dendrites to grow and reach out toward other neurons, but they never touch each other.

The gap between the dendrites is called a synapse. How a synapse functions is extremely important to understanding chemical imbalances and their associated emotional and physical disorders. Again, I will be connecting the dots in Chapter 12. Here is what Wikipedia has to say about synapses, "In the nervous system, a *synapse* is a structure that permits a neuron (or nerve cell) to pass an electrical or chemical signal to another neuron or to the target effector cell."

Going deeper, according to The Brain from Top to Bottom,

> a synapse is the junction point between two neurons. However, a nerve impulse can also be transmitted from a sensory receptor cell to a neuron, or from a neuron to a set of muscles to make them contract, or from a neuron to an endocrine gland to make it secrete a hormone. In these last two cases, the connection points are called neuromuscular and neuroglandular junctions.
>
> In a typical chemical synapse between two neurons, the neuron from which the nerve impulse arrives is called the presynaptic neuron. The neuron to which the neurotransmitters (chemical messengers) bind is called the postsynaptic neuron.
>
> The synaptic gap that the neurotransmitters must cross is very narrow—on the order of 0.02 micron.
>
> Across the gap, the neurotransmitters bind to membrane receptors: large proteins anchored in the cell membrane of the postsynaptic neuron. At this location, under an electron microscope, you can observe an accumulation of opaque material which consists of the

cluster of receptors and other signaling proteins that are essential for chemical neurotransmission.[14]

Key point: simplifying, to get information from one neuron to the next, the data must pass through a gap called the synapse. The transmission of data is controlled by a neurotransmitter. The first step in synaptic transmission is the synthesis and storage of neurotransmitters. Neurotransmitters do not exist naturally; they must be made. Synthesis is the process within our body whereby neurotransmitters are created by combining different types of amino acids. Amino acids are the building blocks of protein. I will show in my second book, Biblical Nutrition, how stress and anxiety cause people to alter their diet with comfort foods limiting their protein intake. The lack of daily protein is at the heart of most chemical imbalances.

Synapse Diagram

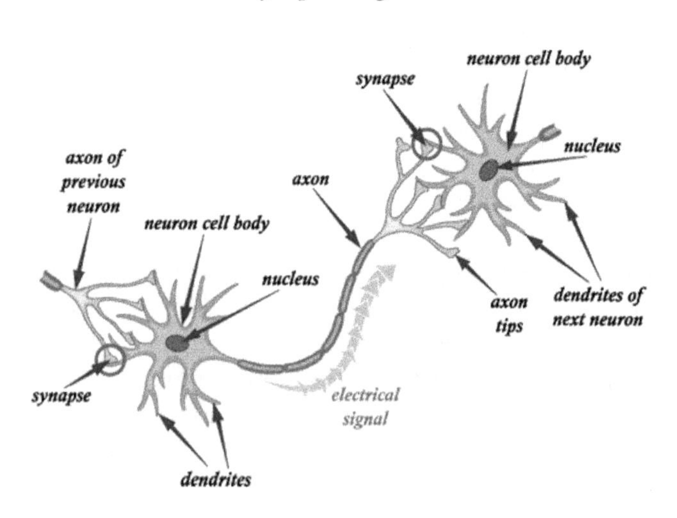

The seventh fresh new revelation

The building blocks of organic life are 22 known amino acids. According to Wikipedia,

> an essential amino acid, or indispensable amino acid, is an amino acid that cannot be synthesized de novo (from scratch) by the organism at a rate commensurate with its demand, and therefore come from the diet. Of the 21 amino acids common to all life forms, the nine amino acids humans cannot synthesize are phenylalanine, valine, threonine, tryptophan, methionine, leucine, isoleucine, lysine, and histidine. Pyrrolysine, considered "the 22nd amino acid," is not used by humans.[15]

Take a wild guess...I will give you three guesses, and the first two do not count: how many letters are in the Jewish alphabet? Correctamundo, there are 22! I can see the evolutionist rolling over in their grave. Probably just a minor coincidence...God has been in control from the moment of creation, and He cannot stop laughing.

This section describes a few of the best-known neurotransmitters that are involved in many functions in both the central and peripheral nervous systems. Apart from acetylcholine, they all belong to the family of amines or amino acids.

Neurotransmitter	*Disorder When is in Short Supply*
Acetylcholine: a very widely distributed excitatory neurotransmitter that triggers muscle contraction and stimulates the excretion of certain hormones. In the central nervous system, it is involved inwakefulness, attentiveness, anger, aggression, sexuality, and thirst, among other things.	Alzheimer's disease is associated with a lack of acetylcholine in certain regions of the brain.

Dopamine: is a neurotransmitter involved in controlling movement and posture. It also modulates mood and plays a central in positive reinforcement and dependency.

The loss of dopamine in certain parts of the brain causes the muscle rigidity typical of Parkinson's disease.

GABA: is an inhibitory neurotransmitter that is very widely distributed in the neurons of the cortex. GABA contributes to motor control, vision, and many other cortical functions.

Some drugs that increase the level of GABA in the brain are used to calm the trembling of people suffering from Huntington's disease.

Glutamate: is a major excitatory a neurotransmitter that is associated with learning and memory.

It is also thought to be associated with Alzheimer's disease, whose first symptoms include memory malfunctions.

Norepinephrine: is a neurotransmitter that is important for attentiveness, emotions, sleeping, dreaming, and learning. Norepinephrine is also released as a hormone into the blood,where it causes blood vessels to contract and heart rate to increase.

Norepinephrine plays a role in mood disorders such as manic depression.

Serotonin: contributes to various functions, such as regulating body temperature, sleep, mood, appetite, and pain.	Depression, suicide, impulsive behavior, and aggressiveness all appear to involve certain imbalances in serotonin.

Practical Examples of Word Generation by Neuro Pathways

If I asked you, "what does 2×2 equal," you would say the word "four." Why and more importantly, where did the word four come from? Right...you repeated the times table to yourself...over and over and over until you memorized it. Neurologically, the act of repeating something over and over (mediating) commits it to long-term memory and creates a neuropathway.

Key point: reinforced neuropathways can last a lifetime. You will remember that 2×2 = 4 for as long as you live. So, the process is: meditation causes dendrites to grow out from a neuron, and they meet up with another neuron with its dendrites, and a neuropathway is formed!

Let us look at another example. Imagine a young child who gets bitten by a dog. In the next (4) weeks of the child's life, every dog the child meets wags its tail and acts friendly. Obviously, the trauma of being bitten would not be reinforced, minimizing the traumatic event.

Conversely, what if in the next (4) weeks of the child's life, every dog the child meets growls and acts aggressively? The traumatic experience of being bitten by the dog would be reinforced negatively causing the child to rehearse the event over and over in its mind. It is the rehearsing of the event that turns it into an everlasting memory (neuropathway).

I think you can easily visualize the type of new conversations going on in this child's mind. This pathway would generate negative words like, "dogs are bad, I am going to get hurt; I need to escape," etc. The words would then lead to thoughts of fear and panic.

Key point: because the traumatic event was rehearsed in the child's mind over and over, it created a neuropathway. Along with it, came words this child had never spoken before in relationship to dogs. Unlike the example of memorizing a times table and its associated neuropathway, this neuropathway is associated with a traumatic event. Physiologically, there are serious ramifications! This child's whole body would be affected by anxiety and stress whenever the child is confronted by a dog. The child, to various degrees, might experience shortness of breath, panic, sweats, etc. Traumatic neuropathways root themselves deeply into a person's entire body, so much so that they can affect the chemical output of our genes. I will go into greater detail regarding how traumatic experiences affect our genetic chemical output in my third book, Death Spiral vs. Life Spiral. The book will provide the science of how the world's way of living creates chemical imbalances within us and how these chemical imbalances control the way we eat and live.

Chapter Summary

The diagram below summarizes what we learned in this chapter! The bigger picture is still somewhat fragmented at this point, but we are moving in the right direction. I guarantee, by the time you read the series of three books, you will be just like me—in total awe of how much God demonstrates His *Love* for us through His Word and His desire to make us whole in every way.

Repetition (meditation)

↓

Grows Dendrites

↓

Creates a New Neuro Pathway and
Becomes a Long-Term Memory

↓

Generates Words Unique to the New Neuropathway

↓

The Newly Created Voice is the Voice of God

↓

Net Result is We Achieve Discernment

The eighth fresh new revelation

Holy Spirit blew me away again! While the above information demonstrates the physiology behind the renewal of our mind, it does not provide the whole picture! Case in point, let's say a person who has never heard of God is evangelized and becomes "Born Again."

Without any prior knowledge of God or His Word, the only voices this person will hear in their mind would be that of the flesh and of the devil (no neuropathways generated by meditating on God's Word). So, on day one of being "Born Again," 99% of conversation in their mind is flesh/devil, and 1% is of God.

As time goes on, assuming this person picks up his/her Bible and reads their Bible, determines the speed at which he/she achieves discernment. Depending on the degree of dedication and meditation put forth is critical and directly proportional to the pace at which the person renews their mind. In my case, because of my desperation (chemical imbalance), I committed to God's Word for an average of 6 hours/day for three years! Effectively, I sped up the process of renewing my mind.

Running out in time, achieving discernment looks like this: the more contact hours a person spends in the Word—new neuropathways are formed. The greater the number of new pathways and reinforcement of those pathways (the speaking of God's Word) is directly proportional to the dominance of His voice in our mind! Once we pass the 50/50 mark, we can be confident the dominant voice we hear will be that of God.

Flesh/Devil's Voice vs.	*God's Voice*
80%	*20%*
70%	*30%*
60%	*40%*
50%	*50%*
40%	*60%*
30%	*70%*
20%	*80%*

The Bible mentions "meditate" or "meditation" 23 times and 19 times in the Book of Psalms. So, let's look at some of those verses.

> This Book of the Law shall not depart from your mouth, but you shall read [and meditate on] it day and night, so that you may be careful to do [everything] in accordance with all that is written in it; for then you will make your way prosperous, and then you will be successful. Have I not commanded you? Be strong and courageous! Do not be terrified or dismayed (intimidated), for the Lord your God is with you wherever you go.
>
> Joshua 1:8-9 (AMP)

> My son, pay attention to my words and be willing to learn; Open your ears to my sayings. Do not let them escape from your sight; Keep them in the center of your heart. For they are life to those who find them, And healing and health to all their flesh.
>
> Proverbs 4:20-22 (AMP)

> Blessed [fortunate, prosperous, and favored by God] is the man who does not walk in the counsel of the wicked [following their advice and example], Nor stand in the path of sinners,

Nor sit [down to rest] in the seat of scoffers (ridiculers). But his delight is in the law of the LORD, And on His law [His precepts and teachings] he [habitually] meditates day and night. And he will be like a tree firmly planted [and fed] by streams of water, Which yields its fruit in its season; Its leaf does not wither; And in whatever he does, he prospers [and comes to maturity]. The wicked [those who live in disobedience to God's law] are not so, But they are like the chaff [worthless and without substance] which the wind blows away. Therefore the wicked will not stand [unpunished] in the judgment, Nor sinners in the assembly of the righteous. For the LORD knows and fully approves the way of the righteous, But the way of the wicked shall perish.

Psalm 1:1-6 (AMP)

Oh, how I love Your law! It is my meditation all the day. Your commandments make me wiser than my enemies, For Your words are always with me. I have better understanding and deeper insight than all my teachers [because of Your word], For Your testimonies are my meditation.

Psalm 119:97-99 (AMP)

The ninth fresh new revelation

Seven in the Bible is always associated with His perfection! Are you ready to be blown away? In the passages above, every time you read meditate or meditation, think, it makes new neuro pathways. This is the physiology of how we renew our mind and generate His voice!

Hopefully, you made it this far. In the next chapter, we will look at the devastation to our health and spiritual growth caused by unforgiveness.

Chapter Eight

The Poison of Unforgiveness

I surely hope by now, you are getting a sense that this book is truly being directed and written by the Holy Spirit. I know I am not this smart and could never take credit for all this wisdom.

Unforgiveness, the greatest detriment to walking in a peace beyond all understanding and soaring high above the pitfalls of life.

This is a very essential chapter. Please take your time reading it... *your reward will be beyond measure!* What you are about to read took me over ten years to learn, and it is one of the main reasons why I am writing this book. You have no idea how I wished I would have known what I am about to share with you.

At the end of this chapter, I will provide you with an easy to follow flow-diagram that will tie together all you are about to discover.

I am going to come at this subject from the following prospectuses.

- Biblically
- Physiologically
- Self-help
- Neurologically
- Epigenetically
- Quantum Physically
- Understanding
- Humility

Biblically

So easy to say, "just forgive him/her/yourself," yet seemingly impossible to do! I promise, by the end of this chapter, you will be well on your way to achieving (it is a process that takes time) a lasting forgiveness towards all those who have hurt you and mostly importantly (if applicable) yourself.

Key point: not forgiving someone or yourself only hurts you! It warps your thinking, affects your behavior, your choices in life, and kills your body. No matter how angry you get about the event(s) that have hurt you so deeply, it does nothing to the other person! They already proved they don't deserve to be in your life!

Worth repeating: you and your health are suffering, not theirs!

Unforgiveness, as a behavior (state of mind/way of thinking), is the *first* change God wants us to make when we begin the process of renewing our mind, freeing us from the binding natures of the flesh and the devil's influence (stinking thinking and bitterness). Need Biblical proof? Let us explore the Biblical account:

The Lord Provides Water

> Then Moses led Israel from the Red Sea, and they went into the Wilderness of Shur; they went [a distance of] three days (about thirty-three miles) in the wilderness and found no water. Then they came to Marah, but they could not drink its waters because they were bitter; therefore it was named Marah (bitter). The people [grew discontented and] grumbled at Moses, saying, "What are we going to drink?" Then he cried to the Lord [for help], and the Lord showed him a tree, [a branch of] which he threw into the waters, and the waters became sweet.
>
> There the Lord made a statute and an ordinance for them, and there He tested them, saying, "If you will diligently listen and pay

attention to the voice of the LORD your God, and do what is right in His sight, and listen to His commandments, and keep [foremost in your thoughts and actively obey] all His precepts and statutes, then I will not put on you any of the diseases which I have put on the Egyptians; for I am the LORD who heals you."

Exodus 15:22-26 (AMP)

Literal Account of Exodus 15:22-26

- Exploring the context of this passage, we see that Israel (approximately 3 million people) was rescued by Moses from the hand of the Egyptians. There is little argument that Egypt is a literal place, and the Israelites were their slaves. As they walked away from the Red Sea, it took them three days before they found a place with water. By then, whatever water they had brought with them had long run out, and they became desperate for water.

- Most people know that as humans, we can only go without water for three days, so, effectively, they were on the edge of death. The first place they came to was a lake. Ironically, a lake whose waters were bitter and could not be drank. Therefore, they named it "Marah" which means bitterness in Hebrew. The Lord then commanded Moses to throw a tree into it and the waters became drinkable.

Symbolic Account of Exodus 15:22-26

Exciting stuff here; please do your best to absorb this as it is vitally important to understanding how God changes us from the inside out neurologically! There is so much going on here symbolically.

- Egypt, in the Bible, is always symbolically associated with the "world" and what it is like to be enslaved by sin and fleshly desires. They worshiped many different gods, wealth, and self-adornment. This slave mentality is devoid of understanding who Jesus (thinking like Him) is and what are the benefits of being in a relationship with Him.

Water, in the Bible, is symbolically associated with the hearing and absorbing of God's Word, mostly referred to as "to drink or drinking the water." This symbology is very similar to what we learned in Chapter 2: "to eat there of the fruit" is the act of adopting a new way of thinking.

> Jesus answered her, "Everyone who drinks this water will be thirsty again. But whoever drinks the water that I give him will never be thirsty again. But the water that I give him will become in him a spring of water [satisfying his thirst for God] welling up [continually flowing, bubbling within him] to eternal life."
>
> John 4:13-14 (AMP)

The symbolic meaning of throwing a "tree" into the water and making it drinkable is to purify the water with Jesus (He is the Word incarnate). Biblically, trees are always associated with life, Jesus, and wisdom. If you were to take the time to underline every time a tree is mentioned in the Bible, you would find that a tree is on the first page of Genesis, in the first Psalm, on the first page of the New Testament, and on the last page of Revelation. Here are just a few Biblical accounts:

The Incarnate Word

> [I am writing about] what existed from the beginning, what we have heard, what we have seen with our eyes, what we have looked at and touched with our hands, concerning the Word of Life [the One who existed even before the beginning of the world, Christ] and the Life [an aspect of His being] was manifested, and we have seen [it as eyewitnesses] and testify and declare to you [the Life], the eternal Life who was [already existing] with the Father and was [actually] made visible to us [His followers] what we have seen and heard we also proclaim to you, so that you too may

have fellowship [as partners] with us. And indeed our fellowship [which is a distinguishing mark of born-again believers] is with the Father, and with His Son Jesus Christ. We are writing these things to you so that our joy [in seeing you included] may be made complete [by having you share in the joy of salvation].

1 John 1:1-4 (AMP)

He gave them another parable [to consider], saying, "The kingdom of heaven is like a mustard seed, which a man took and sowed in his field; and of all the seeds [planted in the region] it is the smallest, but when it has grown it is the largest of the garden herbs and becomes a tree, so that the birds of the air find shelter in its branches."

Matthew 13:31-32 (AMP)

Jesus Is the Vine—Followers Are Branches

I am the true Vine, and My Father is the vinedresser. Every branch in Me that does not bear fruit, He takes away; and every branch that continues to bear fruit, He [repeatedly] prunes, so that it will bear more fruit [even richer and finer fruit]. You are already clean because of the word which I have given you [the teachings which I have discussed with you]. Remain in Me, and I [will remain] in you. Just as no branch can bear fruit by itself without remaining in the vine, neither can you [bear fruit, producing evidence of your faith] unless you remain in Me.

John 15:1-4 (AMP)

The Rewards of Wisdom

For wisdom's profit is better than the profit of silver, And her gain is better than fine gold. She is more precious than rubies; And nothing you can wish for compares with her [in value]. Long life is in her right hand; In her left hand are riches and honor. Her ways are highways of pleasantness and favor, And all her paths are peace. She is a tree of life to those who take hold of her, And happy [blessed, considered fortunate, to be admired] is everyone who holds her tightly.

Proverbs 3:14-18 (AMP)

And he will be like a tree firmly planted [and fed] by streams of water, Which yields its fruit in its season; Its leaf does not wither; And in whatever he does, he prospers [and comes to maturity].

Psalms 1:3 (AMP)

The tenth fresh new revelation

Let us go deep again! Courtesy of Rev. Daryl Sanders. I attended one of his Bible studies in which he was talking about the significance of Marah Lake as the first place the Israelites stopped after exiting Egypt. Spiritually and symbolically speaking, living in Egypt is the same as a person who is not "born again." They are in bondage to sin and the flesh. But when a person accepts Jesus as their Lord and Savior, a process of transition begins changing them from the inside out mentally and physically, as I mentioned in Chapter 6.

When a person becomes born again, they are infused with a thirst for the truth. They need to drink (buy into, believe in) Spiritual water to grow.

This is beautifully depicted in Exodus 15:22-26. The Israelites were desperate for water, but not only for literal water (earthly water); they were also desperate for Spiritual water.

I find it more than coincidental that the first place God brought His people (in the New Testament—born again Christians) was the lake of bitterness (Lake Marah).

Literally, it is a bitter water lake, symbolically—a lesson to be learned. The Israelites were in slavery for over 450 years; they had a slave mentality and were extremely bitter because of this slavery. The same goes for the unbeliever: they have a slave mentality (bitterness).

Beautifully, God is saying here, the first step in the process of change is to understand that earthly water (drinking the water we find on earth, or the earthly way of living) cannot change you...for it is, in essence, a bitter spirit.

To remove the bitterness of earth's water (way of life), we must make the water drinkable (Spiritual/Holy); we must throw a tree into its midst (believe in Jesus). Obviously, from the symbolical perspective, meaning we must learn how to accept Jesus as our Lord and Savior and to think like Him by exposing ourselves to His Word.

Key point: The bitterness mentioned above is synonymous with unforgiveness! Unforgiveness is the practice of engaging in ruminative thoughts of anger, vengeance, hate, and resentment. Additionally, science has now documented that unforgiveness has adverse mental and physical side effects. Unforgiveness affects our well-being, physical health and produces psychological consequences such as emotional instability, cognitive disorders, and behavioral disorders.

Physiologically

Scientific studies (Univ. of Pennsylvania, Article: "Forgiveness: How it Manifests in Our Health, Well-being and Longevity," written by Kathi Norman) have found that unforgiveness can be responsible for elevated blood pressure, vascular resistance, a higher risk of heart attack, increased anxiety, depression, and a decreased immune response. I will clearly show you in Chapters 11 and 12 how the combination of unforgiveness, stress, and anxiety is killing us from the inside by altering the genetic expression of our genes.

Here is another viewpoint from an article I found at theravive.com titled: "The Negative Effects of Unforgiveness on Mental Health." The article was written by Christie Hunter on April 28, 2014.

> Christie Hunter is a registered clinical counselor in British Columbia and co-founder of Theravive. She is a certified management accountant. She has a Master of Arts in counseling psychology from Liberty University with a specialty in marriage and family, and a post-graduate specialty in trauma resolution. In 2007 she started Theravive with her husband to help make mental health care easily attainable and nonthreatening.[16]

Summarizing, unforgiveness is an emotional imbalance caused by a delayed response towards a transgressor. Unforgiveness is a type of stress response and, as such, has a direct impact on the mental health and psychology of a person. Without a resolution, it is a state of mind which confines the unforgiving person to a stressful state of mind.

This confining state of mind often causes a person to take potentially harmful steps, and in extreme cases, people can develop suicidal tendencies.

Below are the most dangerous ways unforgiveness damages our mental health:

- *Chronic Stress Response*. The research study concluded that when a person starts thinking that other people can harm them, it gives rise to negative emotions. Apart from causing severe diseases like cardiovascular issues and high blood pressure, chronic stress can also cause a brain hemorrhage. A person who lets out the negative feelings in the form of hated or violence is less prone to severe health issues than a person who cannot express his/her mental state. Long-term effects of chronic stress can also give rise to psychological disorders. Often persons suffering from chronic stress due to unforgiveness end up as anorexic or bulimic.

- *Short-Term Intense Responses*. This is another common mental health problem that several people go through due to unforgiveness. According to the study of Bauer (2002), short-term unforgiveness provokes a person to respond intensely, which ultimately impacts the social and cognitive behavior of a person. A person suffering from delayed expressions trauma cannot interact with other people. This impacts the communication skills, thinking abilities, and decision-making power of a person. Chi (2001) suggests that the negative effects of unforgiveness are like those of interpersonal mental trauma. Additionally, the trauma caused by unforgiveness can cause the human brain to go into a hyperactive state leading to hormonal imbalances.

- *Depression.* Unaddressed and delayed negative emotions can cause several long-term mental health problems, and depression is one of them. Depression is the most frequently encountered mental health issue, but the depression caused by unexpressed emotions can be more dangerous than other forms. It not only impacts the mental stability of a person but also damages his/her physical health. Common health issues associated with depression that can directly impact mental health are anxiety, short-temperament, and sleeplessness. Moreover, a person suffering from unforgiveness depression cannot trust other people to share his/her feelings, which further triggers negative stressors and worsen the situation.

- *Paranoid Personality Disorder.* According to Carroll (2009), a person suffers from paranoid personality disorder when his/her brain reacts to stressful situations in a hypertensive manner. A person cannot control his/her emotions and therefore struggle to form a firm opinion about any situation. Moreover, in later stages of the disorder, a person can also suffer from hallucinations during a stressful or negative situation. A person suffering from this disorder cannot trust other people and has no or zero self-control. Although the problem is considerably neglected in clinical psychology,

> people suffering from mental setbacks due to unforgiveness probably suffer from a paranoid personality disorder.

Key point: Sadly, God is the last person most people turn to learn how to forgive someone. The world's solution to unforgiveness resulting in poor health, emotional problems, cognitive problems, and behavioral problems is "self-help" material. In fact, according to Marketdata Enterprises, Inc., a leading independent market research publisher since 1979, the self-help industry was estimated as an 11-billion-dollar industry in 2018 and is getting larger every year.

Self-help

As I researched self-help industry articles, it became increasingly obvious that most people who go down this path do not experience lasting change. Apparently, 96% of the people who invested in personal development seminars, courses, set goals and worked on those goals for 90 days, completely failed, according to Srinivas Rao. He is the host and founder of a popular podcast, "The Unmistakable Creative." The show has more than five hundred 5 Star reviews on iTunes and reaches a global market.

Among the many, many other articles I read about the failure of self-help books, I found this one on Quora titled: "Why do many people who read self-help books fail to get results?" which seemed to summarize the industry's lack of success most concisely. The author Matthew Jones put it this way:

> People are exhausted! Mentally, physically, emotionally, and spiritually, people are saturated in their problems, consumed by their limitations, and sulking in their suffering. No matter how much caffeine reaches the bloodstream, blue bags remain under the eyes of my peers, friends, and family. The energy is thick with self-absorption, a basic narcissism enhanced by the voyeuristic tendencies of social media, in which people live out other people's fantasies in one reality, while their own physical body lays

> neglected in the absurdity of life and its treacherous conditions. I wish we could make use of self-help books to escape our self-constructed shackles.[17]

Wow, wow, and wow...are you ready for another Holy Spirit directed revelation?

The eleventh fresh new revelation

Unforgiveness is the reason why people are mentally, physically, emotionally, and spiritually (earthly), saturated in their problems, consumed by their limitations, and sulking in their suffering. The solution is entering into a relationship with Jesus!

It is no wonder why God wants us to address this spiritual condition first. The Bible calls this "the pride of life" (it is all about me). Here are the Biblical accounts:

> For all that is in the world—the lust and sensual craving of the flesh and the lust and longing of the eyes and the boastful *pride of life* [pretentious confidence in one's resources or in the stability of earthly things]—these do not come from the Father, but are from the world.
>
> 1 John 2:16 (AMP)

> Therefore *pride* is their necklace; they clothe themselves with violence.
>
> Psalms 73:6 (NIV)

> When *pride* comes [boiling up with an arrogant attitude of self-importance], then come dishonor and shame, But with the humble [the teachable who have been chiseled by trial and who have learned to walk humbly with God] there is wisdom and soundness of mind.
>
> Proverbs 11:2 (AMP)

Through *pride and* presumption come nothing but strife, But [skillful and godly] wisdom is with those who welcome [well-advised] counsel.

Proverbs 13:10 (AMP)

Pride goes before destruction, And a haughty spirit before a fall.

Proverbs 16:18 (NIV)

He who loves transgression loves strife and is quarrelsome; He who [proudly] raises his gate seeks destruction [because of his arrogant *pride*].

Proverbs 17:19 (AMP)

Haughty and arrogant eyes and a proud heart, The lamp of the wicked [their self-centered *pride*], is sin [in the eyes of God].

Proverbs 21:4 (AMP)

So, if self-help cannot change us...what can? God to the rescue!

Remain in Me, and I [will remain] in you. Just as no branch can bear fruit by itself without remaining in the vine, neither can you [bear fruit, producing evidence of your faith] unless you remain in Me. I am the Vine; you are the branches. The one who remains in Me and I in him bears much fruit, for [otherwise] apart from Me [that is, cut off from vital union with Me] you can do nothing. If anyone does not remain in Me, he is thrown out like a [broken off] branch, and withers and dies; and they gather such branches and throw them into the fire, and they are burned.

John 15:4-6 (AMP)

For it is by grace [God's remarkable compassion and favor drawing you to Christ] that you have been saved [actually delivered from judgment and given eternal life] through faith. And this [salvation] is not of yourselves [not through your own effort], but it is the [undeserved, gracious] gift of God; not as a result of [your] works [nor your attempts to keep the Law], so that no one will [be able to] boast or take credit in any way [for his salvation]. For we are His workmanship [His own master work, a work of art], created in Christ Jesus [reborn from above—spiritually transformed, renewed, ready to be used] for good works, which God prepared [for us] beforehand [taking paths which He set], so that we would walk in them [living the good life which He prearranged and made ready for us].

Ephesians 2:8-10 (AMP)

Therefore if anyone is in Christ [that is, grafted in, joined to Him by faith in Him as Savior], he is a new creature [reborn and renewed by the Holy Spirit]; the old things [the previous moral and spiritual condition] have passed away. Behold, new things have come [because spiritual awakening brings a new life]. But all these things are from God, who reconciled us to Himself through Christ [making us acceptable to Him] and gave us the ministry of reconciliation [so that by our example we might bring others to Him].

2 Corinthians 5:17-18 (AMP)

And I will ask the Father, and He will give you another Helper (Comforter, Advocate, Intercessor—Counselor, Strengthener, Standby), to be with you forever— the Spirit of Truth, whom the world cannot receive [and take to its heart] because it does not see Him or know Him, but you know Him because He (the Holy Spirit) remains with you continually and will be in you. "I will not leave you as orphans [comfortless, bereaved, and helpless]; I will come [back] to you.

John 14:15-18 (AMP)

I can do all things [which He has called me to do] through Him who strengthens and empowers me [to fulfill His purpose—I am self-sufficient in Christ's sufficiency; I am ready for anything and equal to anything through Him who infuses me with inner strength and confident peace.]

Philippians 4:13 (AMP)

Neurologically

Neurological Change (Renewing Our Mind) is Required to Forgive

Obviously, from a Biblical standpoint, change is not only possible... it is guaranteed! But what does that look like scientifically? As part of my research directed by the Holy Spirit, I was led to Dr. Lara Boyd.

Dr. Lara Boyd is a Neuroscientist and Physical Therapist at the University of British Columbia. She is a professor and has held a Canada Research Chair, a Michael Smith Foundation for Health Career Scientist award, and been a Peter Wall Early Career Scholar. Dr. Boyd directs the Brain Behavior Lab at the University of British Columbia. Her TEDx talk, "After watching this, your brain will not be the same," has over 25 million views. Dr. Boyd is an expert in mapping how behaviors, environments, and experiences affect brain health and learning using techniques such as magnetic resonance imaging and non-invasive brain stimulation. To date, this work has largely examined the impact of exercise and learning on neurobiology. In 2020 she was a Wall scholar turning her attention to developing the understanding of how important the arts are for brain health.

Here is a summary of her TEDx talk (which I highly recommend watching). First and foremost, what we know about the brain is changing at a breath-taking pace. Much of what we thought about the brain turns out to be not true or incomplete. *Every time we learn a new fact or skill, we change our brain!*

The technical term for this is called neuroplasticity. Modern inventions like MRI have proven that in the adult brain, all our behaviors change our brain. The data provided by this new technology has shown the brain is in a constant state of change and reorganization, which helps us recover from trauma and damages.

Our brain changes in three very basic ways to support learning; the first is chemical. Our brain transfers chemical signals between the nerve cells via the neurons and triggers a series of actions and reactions. The brain increases the amount of concentration of chemical signaling taking place between the neurons. These rapid chemical changes support short term memory.

The second way the brain changes is by altering its structure by changing the connections between neurons. This takes a bit more time and is therefore related to long term memory.

The third way a brain can change is by altering its function. As we use a brain region more and more, it becomes increasingly excitable and easy to use. These three ways a brain changes can operate separately or in concert with each other. Collectively, they support learning, and they are taking place all the time!

Key point: change is possible and, in fact, is happening all the time! The point is that it takes effort on our behalf to force our brain to alter its function. If you are in the pit of despair like I was, exceedingly addicted, exceedingly depressed to the point of suicide, and want out, continue reading. The big picture being painted here will give you the understanding and tools to affect that change. Again, let us look at how the Bible says this process takes place.

> My son, pay attention to my words and be willing to learn; Open your ears to my sayings. Do not let them escape from your sight; Keep them in the center of your heart. For they are life to those who find them, And healing and health to all their flesh.
>
> Proverbs 4:20-22 (AMP)

> This Book of the Law shall not depart from your mouth, but you shall read [and meditate on] it day and night, so that you may be careful to do [everything] in accordance with all that is written in it; for then you will make your way prosperous, and then you will be successful. Have I not commanded you? Be strong and courageous! Do not be terrified or dismayed (intimidated), for the Lord your God is with you wherever you go.
>
> Joshua 1:8-9 (AMP)

The twelfth fresh new revelation

Proverbs 4:22, "For they are life to those who find them, And healing and health to all their flesh." Breaking it down...healing and health to "all" their flesh. The brain is part of our flesh, so we can be healed! We can learn how to forgive by the "renewing of our mind."

One of the essential elements of the change required to forgive is understanding the relationship between the mind and the brain. The question is, does the brain control the mind, or does the mind control the brain? Researching this, I found that up until around the 1980s, neuroscience believed the brain controlled the mind. That has all changed! There are a significant number of current studies proving the mind is not only separate from the brain, but it, in fact, controls the brain.

Dr. Caroline Leaf gave a TEDx talk, "Science of Thought," which is fascinating. I mentioned her credentials earlier in this book. In the video, she goes into extensive details regarding how neuroscience has evolved and concluded that the mind controls the brain. It turns out, the more we discipline our mind, the more we will change our brain!

The more a person thinks negatively (unforgivingly), the more the brain changes to reinforce the state of mind of unforgiveness. Conversely, the more a person thinks positively (forgivingly), the more the brain changes to reinforce the state of mind of forgiveness. It is called the plastic paradox.

Therefore, the brain is subservient to the mind. Like Henry Ford said, "Whether you think you can or whether you think you cannot... you are right!

So, why is this so important?

At some point in the progression of this methodology of thinking (unforgiveness), it begins to alter our belief system. Later in this chapter, I will show you how our beliefs affect our wellbeing, but it will not make sense without an understanding of a relatively new science called Epigenetics.

Epigenetically

Epigenetics is an emerging field of science that studies heritable changes caused by the activation and deactivation of genes without any change in the underlying DNA sequence of the organism. What in the world does that mean?

Officially, the term epigenetics was first introduced in 1942 by embryologist Conrad Waddington. Quoting from an article that I found at sciencedirect.com titled, "The Origins and Evolution of Epigenetics," here is the summary.

The usage and meaning of the term "epigenetics" have drastically changed since its inception. As recently as the past ten years, evolutionary biologists are now calling for a major revision of Neo-Darwinism. It is now thought that epigenetics is leading to a "paradigm shift" in many fields of biological and medical research such as genetics, development, evolution, cancer, nutrition, and Alzheimer's disease.[18]

One of the pioneers of this new science is Bruce Lipton. According to Wikipedia,

> Lipton received a B.A. in biology from C.W. Post Campus of Long Island University in 1966 and a PhD in developmental biology from the University of Virginia in 1971. From 1973 to 1982, he taught anatomy at the University of Wisconsin School of Medicine, before joining St. George's University School of Medicine as a professor of anatomy for three years. Lipton has said that sometime in the 1980s, he rejected atheism and came to believe that the way cells function demonstrates the existence of God.
>
> From 1987 to 1992, Lipton was involved in research at Pennsylvania State University and Stanford University Medical Center. Since 1993, he has been teaching in non-tenured positions at primarily alternative and chiropractic colleges and schools.

> Lipton has said, "When I first started back in the 70s and my research was coming out, it was the golden age of genes. My research irritated a lot of people. I always thought of them as lemmings running off the cliff of DNA, and I'm standing there on the side with the results from my stem-cell studies thinking, 'Oh my God, you're all going the wrong way.' At some point I realized that they marginalized my work because it did not conform to their conventional beliefs and I thought, well, they are not even being scientists. And I just left the system. I realized the message is more important for the average person than it is to argue in the halls of science."
>
> Lipton has received the 2009 Goi Peace Award.[19]

Simplifying, we need to go back to a revolutionary experiment called the "Placebo Effect." The placebo experiment was the first of its kind to use a double-blind technique. The researchers came up with this great idea to determine the effect of giving sick people a sugar pill instead of actual medicine. They were curious to see what, if any effect, the sugar pill would have.

To guarantee the integrity of the experiment, the researchers did not tell the doctors and the sick patients (double-blind). The results were shocking: people who took the sugar pill actually got healed. This one single experiment has changed the scientific and medical world forever!

Summarizing from the video on YouTube, "Epigenetics – How Does it Work" by Bruce Lipton, the placebo effect has resulted in the medical understanding that our beliefs/perceptions can change the expression of our genes positively and negatively. Reluctantly, medical science has been forced to admit that some spontaneous remissions are directly tied to people having a profound change in their perceptions or beliefs about life.

Key point: Not only does this demonstrate just how much God loves us, remember, we are designed in His image. To me, it clearly provides proof He gave us the ability to heal ourselves when our beliefs are aligned with His Words! Here are just a few Biblical accounts.

> Then they cried out to the Lord in their trouble, And He saved them from their distresses. He sent His word and healed them, And rescued them from their destruction. Let them give thanks to the Lord for His lovingkindness, And for His wonderful acts to the children of men!
>
> Psalms 107:19-21 (AMP)

> Lord my God, I cried to You for help, and You healed me.
>
> Psalms 30:2 (NIV)

> When the righteous cry [for help], the LORD hears And rescues them from all their distress and troubles. The LORD is near to the heartbroken And He saves those who are crushed in spirit (contrite in heart, truly sorry for their sin). Many hardships and perplexing circumstances confront the righteous, But the LORD rescues him from them all. He keeps all his bones; Not one of them is broken. Evil will cause the death of the wicked, And those who hate the righteous will be held guilty and will be condemned. The LORD redeems the soul of His servants, And none of those who take refuge in Him will be condemned.
>
> Psalms 34:17-22 (AMP)

> Bless and affectionately praise the Lord, O my soul, And do not forget any of His benefits; Who forgives all your sins, Who heals all your diseases; Who redeems your life from the pit, Who crowns you [lavishly] with lovingkindness and tender mercy.
>
> Psalms 103:2-4 (AMP)

In the video (which I highly recommend you watching...it is only 6 minutes and 45 seconds), Bruce Lipton points out that Jesus said you can renew health by renewing your mind. Here are the Biblical accounts:

> My son, pay attention to my words and be willing to learn; Open your ears to my sayings. Do not let them escape from your sight; Keep them in the center of your heart. For they are life to those who find them, And healing and health to all their flesh.
>
> Proverbs 4:20-22 (AMP)

> He saved us, not because of any works of righteousness that we have done, but because of His own compassion and mercy, by the cleansing of the new birth (spiritual transformation, regeneration) and renewing by the Holy Spirit.
>
> Titus 3:5 (AMP)

> And do not be conformed to this world [any longer with its superficial values and customs], but be transformed and progressively changed [as you mature spiritually] by the renewing of your mind [focusing on godly values and ethical attitudes], so that you may prove [for yourselves] what the will of God is, that which is good and acceptable and perfect [in His plan and purpose for you].
>
> Romans 12:2 (AMP)

> Therefore we do not become discouraged [spiritless, disappointed, or afraid]. Though our outer self is [progressively] wasting away, yet our inner self is being [progressively] renewed day by day.
>
> 2 Corinthians 4:16 (AMP)

> Even youths grow weary and tired, And vigorous young men stumble badly, But those who wait for the LORD [who expect, look for, and hope in Him] Will gain new strength and renew their power; They will lift up their wings [and rise up close to

> God] like eagles [rising toward the sun]; They will run and not become weary, They will walk and not grow tired.
>
> Isaiah 40:30-31 (AMP)

Amazing, but are there any limitations to our God-given power to change? The *only* limitations to our God-given ability to heal ourselves are the limitations of the environment we live in. For it is the beliefs of the people we surround ourselves with that influence our perception, and since perception controls our physiology (epigenetics), it stands to reason the philosophy of others can either support our healing or degrade it.

Our perceptions (biblically, our faith) are literally fields of powerful energy for change. These fields of energy are equally powerful in either direction: while a positive thought (our faith in Jesus) can heal us, a negative thought (our faith in the world's way of living, i.e., beliefs/medicines/doctors) can make us sick or kill us. Such is the power of our thought life that controls our physiology! I hear you; you want the Biblical account.

> And He could not do a miracle there at all [because of their unbelief] except that He laid His hands on a few sick people and healed them.
>
> Mark 6:5 (AMP)

> And He did not do many miracles there because of their lack of faith.
>
> Matthew 13:58 (NIV)

So, why couldn't Jesus do miracles in His own hometown?

The thirteenth fresh new revelation

The reason why Jesus could not do miracles in His hometown was that the people who saw Him grow up did not believe in Him! There was no field of energy to produce the change. Important to note here: the beliefs of those around us can supersede our God-given right to be healed through their negative influences affecting your ability to express your own beliefs.

Therefore, our greatest limitations are the cultural beliefs we buy into because everyone else shares them. An example of this can be seen in every ghetto worldwide. Personally, until my experience with the Holy Spirit, I could not understand why people would continue to live in a ghetto. Even though they are poor beyond imagination, most either have a TV or access to TV. They can see other people live better than they do and quite possibly have heard of the many who have risen out of the ghetto to become rich and famous! Granted, from a percentage standpoint, the number of people who rise above is very small, but does not change the fact that it can be done.

Through my understanding of epigenetics, I now know why most people living in ghetto stay there. Ghetto life is a spirit (state of mind, a way of thinking) that can be defined as a cultural belief of failure and poverty. They are consciously and/or subconsciously reinforcing the belief that this is their fate, and nothing can be done about it. Sadly, it is only on rare occasions a person rises above the cultural beliefs(spirit) of failure and poverty that everyone around them is buying into and breaks free.

Key point: if you are as fascinated by epigenetics as I am, Bruce Lipton has many videos on YouTube you can explore. Additionally, I highly recommend watching this epigenetic video on YouTube: "Epigenetics Influencing Health Outcomes." The video (only 5 minutes and 40 seconds) is produced by The Metagenics Healthcare Institute for Clinical Nutrition.

Metagenics Institute is a trusted, peer-to-peer, evidence-based educational resource for nutrition and personalized medicine. In their video, they elaborate very effectively on the difference between

DNA and the genes that make up our DNA by using an example of identical twins.

As identical twins, they have the same DNA, the genetic information stored in their cells that serves as a code that tells their bodies how to function. The DNA determines what the genes do, the chemicals they produce, and what health risks they are predisposed to throughout their lives.

Even though the twins are identical, they are not alike in their personalities and behaviors or their health as they age. One gains weight, while the other maintains a healthy weight. The one who gained weight develops cardiovascular disease while the other does not. If they have the same DNA, how can that happen?

DNA is not our *destiny!* Through epigenetics, new evidence is now emerging, proving we can change the effect of our genetic makeup on our health.

Summarizing: prior to 1985, medical science was telling everyone that the reason why people get diseases and cancers is because they have a predisposition to do so. Effectively, there is something wrong with their DNA. As a result, they were telling people, "if your parents had cancer, then you have a greater risk of having cancer. If your parents were alcoholics, then you have a predisposition to becoming an alcoholic."

The study of epigenetics has more than clinically proven this to be wrong. We now know there has never been anything wrong with our DNA. The problem that causes diseases, alcoholism and/or cancers to manifest is the readout of our genes. Gene readout is affected by two processes within our bodies: histone modification and DNA methylation. These are very complex processes and would require hundreds of pages to explain, so I think it would be best (if you are so inclined) to do your own research, so I can keep things simple and on point. Important to keep in mind: I am painting a unique picture of how God changes us from the inside out from a neurological standpoint. Referencing these sciences is only part of that picture!

Key point: most people do not realize the human body is its own chemistry set, constantly taking raw elements like amino acids and chemically combining them within the body to make very complex chemical compounds. As is in the case with the DNA methylation cycle, several nutrients are required like Vitamin B12, Vitamin B6, and Folic Acid. If these raw elements are lacking (not at optimal levels) from our diet, the DNA methylation process will be affected. We now know that when the DNA methylation process is interrupted, diseases like cancer, cardiovascular, Alzheimer's, and diabetes can develop.

To simplify, genes have a positive switch and a negative switch. When a gene's positive switch is triggered, the chemical output of that specific gene promotes health. When a gene's negative switch is triggered, the chemical output of that specific gene degrades our health. So, this begs the question: what is the triggering mechanism? I will answer that question in Chapter 8.

The fourteenth fresh new revelation

This is a big one! I have been promising all along to wow you, so here we go! Admittedly, I am getting ahead of myself here, but I want to keep you motivated to continue reading. I will be going into much more detail in Chapter 11.

The word "vitamin" is an acronym that stands for "vital amino acids." The reason why some vitamins are vital is that the only way we can obtain them is through diet. So, why is this so important, and where is the great revelation?

To grasp the totality of the revelation, you need to know the human mind is estimated to perform 100,000 chemical reactions per second. Yes, I said per second. Additionally, it is estimated that across the entire human body, we are performing 37 thousand billion billion (that is a 37 with 21 zeros after it) chemical reactions per second...I told you, our body is its own chemistry set.

Starting to get excited? Maybe not...Okay, let's go deeper! The reason why B vitamins specifically are so important is because every one of these chemical reactions requires the presence of one or more B vitamins. So, what is so special about that, you may ask.

Drum roll...Without the proper balance of B vitamins obtained through our diet, the body cannot do the chemistry needed to keep us healthy and emotionally stable! While this is a major piece of information, the rest of this revelation, which can be found in Chapter 11, completely blew me away.

Quantum Physically

Being considerate of your time, I am going to briefly touch base on one of the primary laws of quantum physics called Entanglement. This aspect of quantum physics speaks to the universality of the poison of unforgiveness. If you would like to spend more time understanding this fascinating science, I would highly recommend reading the following books written in laymen's language: *Parallel Universes* by Fred Alan Wolf and *The Dancing Wu Li Master – An Overview of the New Physics* by Gary Zukav.

As we learned earlier, beliefs are fields of energy. As a field of energy, it radiates outwardly from us and affects the people around us. Fundamentally, unforgiveness is a belief wherein we believe it is our right to seek revenge on the person who hurt us, and they need to be punished. By definition: *unforgiveness is the practice of engaging in ruminative thoughts of anger, vengeance, hate, and resentment.*

According to Wikipedia,

> Quantum entanglement is a physical phenomenon that occurs when a pair or group of particles are generated, interact, or share spatial proximity in a way such that the quantum state of each particle of the pair or group cannot be described independently of the state of the others, including when the particles are separated by a large distance.[20]

The poison of unforgiveness is universal because all people, whether they realize it or not, are in a relationship with one another. Every single person on this planet is in a quantum physics entanglement relationship with each other. Sub-atomically, everything touches everything. As such, not only does unforgiveness damage "us" mentally and physically; through the understanding of quantum entanglement, we also now know it affects the whole universe.

Summarizing, when two particles (we are made of particles) are in a relationship, no matter how far apart from each other they are, they still affect each other.

So easy to say, "just forgive him/her/yourself," yet seemingly impossible to do! Having finally arrived on the other shore Spiritually (born again) and having received the peace beyond understanding, I pray that this book is somehow instrumental in expediting your procurement of the same peace.

Do not be like me, who had to die to live! Jesus is real; God is real and the Holy Spirit. The Word of God...is life-breathed, and it *will* change your life.

Prior to my death, I was a person who knew about God, read the Bible cover to cover three times, and believed in God, but my heart was still hardened. I was still conformed to the mindset from the tree of the knowledge of good and evil. Do good, get good, if you do bad to me...boy, were you going to get bad from me!

Ironically, even though I knew God, I had no concept of being in a relationship with Him. Reflecting, I now realize my knowledge of God back then was head (brain) knowledge shaped by the worldly point of view: God is just sitting up in heaven waiting for me to make a mistake so He can justify hitting me with a lightning bolt, break my leg or even worse, as most still believe today, *Give me cancer to humble me!*

> "This is the covenant that I will make with them After those days, says the Lord:
>
> I will imprint My laws upon their heart, And on their mind I will inscribe them [producing an inward change]," He then says,

> "And their sins and their lawless acts I will remember no more [no longer holding their sins against them]." Now where there is [absolute] forgiveness and complete cancellation of the penalty of these things, there is no longer any offering [to be made to atone] for sin.
>
> Hebrews 10:16-18 (AMP)

Wow, wow, and wow...again. *Nothing* could be further from the truth! I now hang out with God, Jesus, and the Holy Spirit continually and cannot imagine life without them. Tears of joy can be seen on my face occasionally, my smile is ever-present, and my body is almost always in a state of rest.

So, if you allow me to plant some more seeds with you, I would be greatly honored. An article I found on huffpost.com titled, "Let Your Heart Talk to Your Brain," by Deborah Rozman, confirmed to me God's Words are so much more than just words. *All* the Words of God are not only life-breathed; they prove God is the Ultimate Physiologist!

Deborah Rozman is a psychologist with 30 years of experience. She is the president and CEO of HeartMath Inc. and HeartMath parent company Quantum Intech, Inc., which oversees strategic alliances and the expansion of HeartMath technologies internationally. Rozman sits on and has memberships with many boards and organizations. Among these are the Transformational Leadership Council, the Advisory Board of the Transformative Technology Lab, HMI's Scientific Advisory Board and Physics of Humanity council, and the Global Coherence Initiative Steering Committee. She is also a regular columnist with the Huffington Post.

Here is what the article says:

> When I was a practicing psychologist, sometimes when I'd be working with a client who was confused about an issue or decision, I'd ask, "What would your heart say?" I often adapted a gestalt technique using two chairs. When the client was sitting in one chair, I asked them to speak from their heart and talk to their

mind sitting over there in the other chair. Then I would have them switch chairs and speak from their head, talking to their heart, telling their heart the mind's views and concerns.

It was like two different people talking. The heart spoke from genuine feeling and authenticity, in the present. The mind spoke from opinions, fears, shoulds and shouldn'ts. I had them switch chairs several times, until they had an epiphany. Very often the client would realize their heart's voice was their true self, a voice that offered both more intuition and common-sense intelligence.

This is no coincidence. What is fascinating is that the heart contains a little brain in its own right. Yes, the human heart, in addition to its other functions, possesses a heart-brain composed of about 40,000 neurons that can sense, feel, learn, and remember. The heart-brain sends messages to the head brain about how the body feels and more. When I first heard about this scientific research, it intuitively made sense. I had felt for a long time that the heart has its own mysterious way of knowing.[21]

The fifteenth fresh new revelation

One of the reasons why I believe the Holy Spirit directed me to write this book was because science, although it has a long, long way to go to catch up with God's wisdom, has finally made enough discoveries to validate how God's Word changes us from the inside out neurologically. Did you know that the word "brain" is not mentioned in the Bible? Yet, the word "heart" is cited 826 times! This unique journey the Holy Spirit has me on continuously shows me the physiological undertones in every scripture I read.

To me, and my sincere prayer is that after reading this book, you will also see, it makes all the sense in the world that God's Spiritual Words need to be written to our heart-brain as opposed to our head-brain. The reason being, as stated above, the head-brain only sees life through rose-

colored glasses. Meaning, it is tainted by corrupted information like opinions, fears, shoulds and shouldn'ts.

It sounds a lot like what we learned about the curse of the knowledge of good vs. evil. I know, by now, you are craving the Biblical accounts. Obviously, with 826 appearances, I will be only sharing a small sampling with you.

> "Behold, the days are coming," says the Lord, "when I will make a new covenant with the house of Israel (the Northern Kingdom) and with the house of Judah (the Southern Kingdom), not like the covenant which I made with their fathers in the day when I took them by the hand to bring them out of the land of Egypt, My covenant which they broke, although I was a husband to them," says the Lord. "But this is the covenant which I will make with the house of Israel after those days," says the Lord, "I will put My law within them, and I will write it on their hearts; and I will be their God, and they will be My people. And each man will no longer teach his neighbor and his brother, saying, 'Know the Lord,' for they will all know Me [through personal experience], from the least of them to the greatest," says the Lord. "For I will forgive their wickedness, and I will no longer remember their sin."
>
> Jeremiah 31:31-34 (AMP)

> Moreover, I will give you a new heart and put a new spirit within you, and I will remove the heart of stone from your flesh and give you a heart of flesh.
>
> Ezekiel 36:26 (AMP)

> Create in me a pure heart, O God, And renew a steadfast spirit within me.
>
> Psalm 51:10 (NIV)

> You are our letter [of recommendation], written in our hearts, recognized and read by everyone. You show that you are a letter from Christ, delivered by us, written not with ink but with the

Spirit of the living God, not on tablets of stone but on tablets of human hearts.

2 Corinthians 3:2-3 (AMP)

A happy heart is good medicine and a joyful mind causes healing, But a broken spirit dries up the bones.

Proverbs 17:22 (AMP)

Bind them on your fingers; write them on the tablet of your heart.

Proverbs 7:3 (NIV)

Take delight in the Lord, and He will give you the desires of your heart.

Psalm 37:4 (NIV)

Trust in and rely confidently on the Lord with all your heart And do not rely on your own insight or understanding. In all your ways know and acknowledge and recognize Him, And He will make your paths straight and smooth [removing obstacles that block your way].

Proverbs 3:5-6 (AMP)

And the peace of God [that peace which reassures the heart, that peace] which transcends all understanding, [that peace which] stands guard over your hearts and your minds in Christ Jesus [is yours].

Philippians 4:7 (AMP)

This next Holy Spirit directed wisdom came by way of Bishop TD Jakes. He does not know this because we have never met, but his sermons saved my life! My depression with suicidal thoughts for three years was so consuming and filled with a gigantic sense of worthlessness. I had no hope. I cried myself to sleep for most of those nights. Sometimes the emotional pain was so great I wanted to smash my head into the wall to make it go away.

It was the combination of his and the other pastors I listed in the introduction and hundreds and hundreds of hours of listening to their sermons that brought me back to life over and over.

There are two sermons I found on YouTube: "Let It Go" held at Zion Church (32 minutes) and "Finding Freedom the Faith to Forgive," parts 1, 2, and 3, that changed my life so profoundly. I will never be the same. Yup, it is all about forgiveness. The following comments are paraphrases from these videos.

Forgiveness is a *big* idea! It is for people who are *big* enough to see the *big* picture. It is not for little people. If you research the success stories of people who have risen to the top of their respective professions, you will notice a pattern. What makes them different is the way they handle problems. They see problems from a proper perspective!

They always take the high road; they think like eagles. Conversely, little people think like chickens. Chickens forage on the ground, eating things like corn, sticks, and occasionally the feces they drop. Obviously, feces are what should have been released, not eaten. If a person continues to eat that which should be released, it weighs them down. So, no matter how much you flap and flutter, you can only go so high because of what you have been eating (remember, to eat of something is to institute that state of mind, activate the associated neuropathways).

Paradoxically, when a person has unforgiveness, they are eating what they should have excreted. If you eat like chicken, you cannot fly like an eagle. Eagles eat in high places; they do not eat feces. The eyes of an eagle are keen, and they can see for miles. They soar thousands and thousands of feet high and therefore could never mate with a chicken. Chickens cannot fly that high.

We all need to be promoted to the next level, but we will not reach that next level if we keep eating what is on the ground. Applying what we have learned about neuropathways, if we keep bringing up in our mind the same painful memories, the same issues, old stuff that should have been over with, the night of the living dead, we reinforce the associated pathways and turn them into superhighways. The voice of the superhighway pathway will play over and over in our mind killing you from the inside out.

Key point: our brain is changing all the time, so why is it so hard to forgive? The key to the answer lies in the third way our brain changes. Repetition! It is the repetition of an event that makes its associated neuropathway increasingly excitable and easier to use/access. To help you better understand this process, let us look at the trauma of someone breaking our heart.

By way of example: broken hearts are common to all people. When someone breaks our heart, what do we do? Initially, we think about it (meditate) virtually every minute of every day for weeks, months, and even years. Not only do we think about it over and over, reinforcing the neuropathway associated with the traumatic experience, we tell everyone we meet how so and so hurt us.

In the very same way, we all used repetition (mediation) to teach ourselves the times table. Verbalizing to everyone we meet about how our heart was broken grows those neuropathways into major highways creating life-long long-term memories!

The thinking and speaking (meditation) of the trauma reinforces the pathway to such an extent it produces a louder and louder inner voice constantly playing the same broken record over and over, and without a counterbalance (God's Word), it will not ever leave us!

And therein lies the reason why forgiveness is so hard to achieve. Through the process of meditation on the negative, we simply cannot just forget what that person did to us because we have this ever-present internal voice reminding us of the event(s).

Unforgiveness keeps people in the chicken coop, but God is calling us to the mountain. It is important to note whatever we let control us becomes our master and will ruin us or promote us. Our memories (negative neuropathways), our pains, our scares, and abuse, for the unforgiving person, becomes our master. Effectively, it turns us into a slave. If a certain person walks into a room and changes your mood, you are a slave!

You might be at the grocery store, turn down a new aisle and see "her," and if your whole mood changes, you have not forgiven her. Unforgiveness turns out is a learned behavior. It is not present in animals; they do not bite you because they are angry with you. It is not present in babies. It is not present in young children. Kids commonly get into fights and then, a few minutes later, forgive each other, but their parents will hold a grudge for years. If it is not in animals, babies, and young children, where does it come from? We learn it from life experiences!

The title of this chapter is "The Poison of Unforgiveness." Not forgiving someone is like you drinking poison and waiting for the other person to die. It has no effect on the other person, but if you keep it up, you surely will.

Let us go a bit deeper. Does unforgiveness protect a person from getting hurt again? No, it is not a force field. Another side effect of unforgiveness that people tend to overlook is how it affects their future. Unforgiving people allow their history to alter their destiny, just like cancer kills us from the inside. Their unresolved history is killing their destiny.

Conversely, God has a plan for your life that your eyes have not seen, and your ears have not heard, nor has it entered into your heart. He promises to those who follow Him that their latter days will be their *best*, happiest, and freest days. But He cannot give us this future when our hands are full of the past. In essence, we must let go of where we have been so that we can seize where we are about to go! By letting go of the past, we become energized with a beautiful sense of freedom. For it is the energy of being free from the past that empowers us to walk into our new destiny.

It is time to release from where you have been and spread your wings like eagles and fly soaring high above the chicken mentality. As always, let us look at the Biblical account.

Jesus said to His disciples, "Stumbling blocks [temptations and traps set to lure one to sin] are sure to come, but woe (judgment is coming) to him through whom they come! It would be better for him if a millstone [as large as one turned by a donkey] were hung around his neck and he were hurled into the sea, than for him to cause one of these little ones to stumble [in sin and lose faith]. Pay attention and always be on guard [looking out for one another]! If your brother sins and disregards God's precepts, solemnly warn him; and if he repents and changes, forgive him. Even if he sins against you seven times a day, and returns to you seven times and says, 'I repent,' you must forgive him [that is, give up resentment and consider the offense recalled and annulled]."

The apostles said to the Lord, "Increase our faith [our ability to confidently trust in God and in His power]." And the Lord said, "If you have [confident, abiding] faith in God [even as small] as a mustard seed, you could say to this mulberry tree [which has very strong roots], 'Be pulled up by the roots and be planted in the sea'; and [if the request was in agreement with the will of God] it would have obeyed you.

Luke 17:1-6 (AMP)

Literal Account of Luke 17:1-6

- All the Words in these passages are literal. The advice given here is straight forward: *offenses will come*. But God will take care of the people in our life who cause us to stumble by offending us. In fact, God put this promise in His Word.

If possible, as far as it depends on you, live at peace with everyone. Beloved, never avenge yourselves, but leave the way open for God's wrath [and His judicial righteousness]; for it is written [in Scripture], "Vengeance is Mine, I will repay," says the Lord. But if your enemy is hungry, feed him; if he is thirsty, give him a drink; for by doing this you will heap burning coals on his head.

Romans 12:18-20 (AMP)

- I want to draw your attention to the type of tree mentioned in verse 6, the "mulberry" tree. With all the hours I have spent reading God's Word, I can tell you beyond a shadow of a doubt, every Word is there for a reason!

- So why did God choose a mulberry tree? It turns out that the mulberry tree's root system is very vigorous. Uniquely, most of its roots grow horizontally outward as opposed to vertically downward (see picture below). This type of root growth is very strong and tends to dominate the surrounding soil areas.

Symbolic Account of Luke 17:1-6

- Symbolically, here we are again talking about a tree. Everything we have learned about trees in the previous chapters applies. The paradox here is while this tree does give life, it provides shade and fruit; its root system, though, overshadows the surrounding area and takes life. Spiritually, this is a picture of the poison of unforgiveness.

- Neurologically, the symbolism is how strong and horizontally rooted (many neuropathways) unforgiveness can become. The bitterness of unforgiveness roots itself deep into our soil, and left unresolved, spreads very aggressively not only within us but also vigorously outwardly. The outward nature of these roots touches the people in our inner circle. Physiologically, this causes great amounts of stress and anxiety for them and us and is slowly killing us and them from the inside.

- The horizontal symbolism of these roots speaks to the far-reaching (horizontal) nature of any person with unforgiveness. Remember, unforgiving people are angry and hateful people. Sadly, they usually hurt the people who surround them, their immediate family, and friends, which usually leads to additional horizontal collateral damage. Left unchecked, it can spiral out of control, infecting many, many people and potentially can manifest into racialism.

The Root System of the Mulberry Tree

Forgiveness 101

As promised, here is what forgiveness looks like. The recipe for the process of forgiveness contains three ingredients: the heart-brain resolution, the head-brain resolution, and humility resolution.

The heart-brain resolution. It is God, Jesus, and the Holy Spirit's responsibility to work within us to remove the dead branches, prune the good branches, and replace our hardened heart with a new heart. Willpower cannot do it, nor can self-help. The only thing required on our behalf is to remain connected to them, i.e., meditate on the Word!

> Blessed [anticipating God's presence, spiritually mature] are the pure in heart [those with integrity, moral courage, and godly character], for they will see God.
>
> Matthew 5:8 (AMP)

The word "pure" in this verse, in the Greek, is cathartic or medically...a catheter. A catheter is inserted to drain out impurities. This device is a passive piece of equipment; it functions on its own. As impurities are generated within the body, they are immediately flushed out through the catheter. No decision or mental effort is required. Impurities (offenses) do come, but when we are in a true relationship with God, Jesus, and Holy Spirit, collectively, They become the flushing mechanism. Their purity transforms us through a cathartic cleansing. This Spiritual flushing pushes out that which we do not need and allows us to hold onto that which we do need.

Blessed are the pure in heart! As unbelievers with little or no Godly produced neuropathways generating God's voice as a counterbalance, our hearts are anything but pure. Only through the repetitiveness (meditation on God's Word) of *reading* God's Word does our heart begin the process of cleansing, leading to a softened heart.

Here is the Biblical account.

> For the word of God is living and active and full of power [making it operative, energizing, and effective]. It is sharper than any two-edged sword, penetrating as far as the division of the soul and spirit [the completeness of a person], and of both joints and marrow [the deepest parts of our nature], exposing and judging the very thoughts and intentions of the heart.
>
> Hebrews 4:12 (AMP)

> I am the true Vine, and My Father is the vinedresser. Every branch in Me that does not bear fruit, He takes away; and every branch that continues to bear fruit, He [repeatedly] prunes, so that it will bear more fruit [even richer and finer fruit]. You are already clean because of the word which I have given you [the teachings which I have discussed with you]. Remain in Me, and I [will remain] in you. Just as no branch can bear fruit by itself without remaining in the vine, neither can you [bear fruit, producing evidence of your faith] unless you remain in Me. I am the Vine; you are the branches. The one who remains in Me and I in him bears much fruit, for [otherwise] apart from Me [that is, cut off from vital union with Me] you can do nothing. If anyone does not remain in Me, he is thrown out like a [broken off] branch, and withers and dies; and they gather such branches and

> throw them into the fire, and they are burned. If you remain in Me and My words remain in you [that is, if we are vitally united and My message lives in your heart], ask whatever you wish and it will be done for you. My Father is glorified and honored by this, when you bear much fruit, and prove yourselves to be My [true] disciples.
>
> John 15:1-8 (AMP)

The *head-brain resolution* requires a reason/logic produced solution. This solution is obtained through the process of understanding. We have conclusively learned that once a neuropathway has been created through the process of meditation, it is a life-long event. The longevity of negative pathways makes forgiveness seemly impossible. *Understanding* is the bridge that bypasses the negative pathways!

The sixteenth fresh new revelation

This one gives me goosebumps! Courtesy of TD Jakes...the secret to forgiveness is understanding the person who hurt us. We need to make a distinction between weakness and wickedness. He might have been weak, but he was not wicked; she might have been weak, but she was not wicked. The irony is we think these people are doing this to us, but the truth is they are doing it to themselves. Yes, we were the victim of their weakness, but is it not arrogant of us to think we do not have any weaknesses of our own? The Biblical account is very clear.

> Blessed [content, sheltered by God's promises] are the merciful, for they will receive mercy.
>
> Matthew 5:7 (AMP)

There is not a person who has lived...if they are honest with themselves, who at some point in their life knew, that they knew they needed mercy. Needing mercy is a declaration we are/were guilty of something. Think of it this way: if we are accused of a crime we did not commit, when we go to court, we want justice. Justice is the friend of the innocent, therefore, we would pray for justice!

Interestingly, when we are accused of something for which we are guilty, we pray for mercy. As Christian believers, we know we are forgiven by God through His mercies, the life of Jesus, and His death for our sins. We did not deserve it; it is the gift of God's mercy. So, our arrogance is: how can we be mercifully forgiven and then turn around and not mercifully forgive others?

I can hear some of you saying, "now wait for a cotton-picking-minute there, mister, if you truly knew the extent to which so and so hurt me, there would be no doubt in 'anyone's' mind he/she is guilty!" I hate to burst your bubble, so are you (for something)?

Key point: at the end of the day, what remains is: unresolved unforgiveness does nothing to the person who hurt us, and its poison is slowly spreading outward to our circle of family and friends. Left unresolved, it is slowly killing us and those around us. If God has ever forgiven you, though you were guilty, had mercy on you even when you were wrong, and you want to be free from the pit of depression created by unforgiveness—let it go!

The *humility resolution* also requires an element of understanding! In a way, unforgiveness is a form of self-justification (what we believe is our right to seek revenge) whereby our pride has been hurt by a transgressor. Perhaps this will make it even clearer: a person is only unforgiving because they have a prideful spirit. Conversely, a person full of humility and gratefulness has a much greater chance at forgiving people and/or their self because true humility leads to a greater degree of understanding one's own self-worth.

Key point: we must be careful here, as there are two definitions of humility! The world's definition and the biblical definition. According to Wikipedia, the world's definition is

> a low self-regard and sense of unworthiness. Humility is an outward expression of an appropriate inner, or self-regard, and is contrasted with humiliation, which is an imposition, often external, of shame upon a person. Humility may be misappropriated as ability to suffer humiliation through self-denouncements which remains focused on self rather than low self-focus.
>
> Humility, in various interpretations, is widely seen as a virtue which centers on low self-preoccupation, or unwillingness to put oneself forward, so it is in many religious and philosophical traditions, it contrasts with narcissism, hubris and other forms of pride and is an idealistic and rare intrinsic construct that has an extrinsic side.[22]

Conversely, the biblical definition of humility is having a realistic view of one's importance and reverent worship of God. According to Rabbi Lord Jonathan Sacks,

> in Judaism humility is an appreciation of oneself, one's talents, skills, and virtues. It is not meekness or self-deprecating thought, but the effacing of oneself to something higher. Humility is not to think lowly of oneself, but to appreciate the self, one has received. In recognition of the mysteries and complexities of life, one becomes humbled to the awesomeness of what one is and what one can achieve.[23]

Quite the contrast! Besides increasing our ability to forgive, the value of humility is great; here are a few Biblical accounts:

> The [reverent] fear of the Lord [that is, worshiping Him and regarding Him as truly awesome] is the instruction for wisdom [its starting point and its essence]; And before honor comes *humility.*
>
> Proverbs 15:33 (AMP)

Before disaster the heart of a man is haughty *and* filled with self-importance, But *humility* comes before honor.

Proverbs 18:12 (AMP)

The reward of *humility* [that is, having a realistic view of one's importance] and the [reverent, worshipful] fear of the Lord Is riches, honor, and life.

Proverbs 22:4 (AMP)

With all *humility* [forsaking self-righteousness], and gentleness [maintaining self-control], with patience, bearing with one another in [unselfish] love.

Ephesians 4:2 (AMP)

Do nothing from selfishness or empty conceit [through factional motives, or strife], but with [an attitude of] *humility* [being neither arrogant nor self-righteous], regard others as more important than yourselves.

Philippians 2:3 (AMP)

Have this same attitude in yourselves which was in Christ Jesus [look to Him as your example in selfless *humility*].

Philippians 2:5 (AMP)

Chapter Summary

Below is the diagram that ties all the components of forgiveness together:

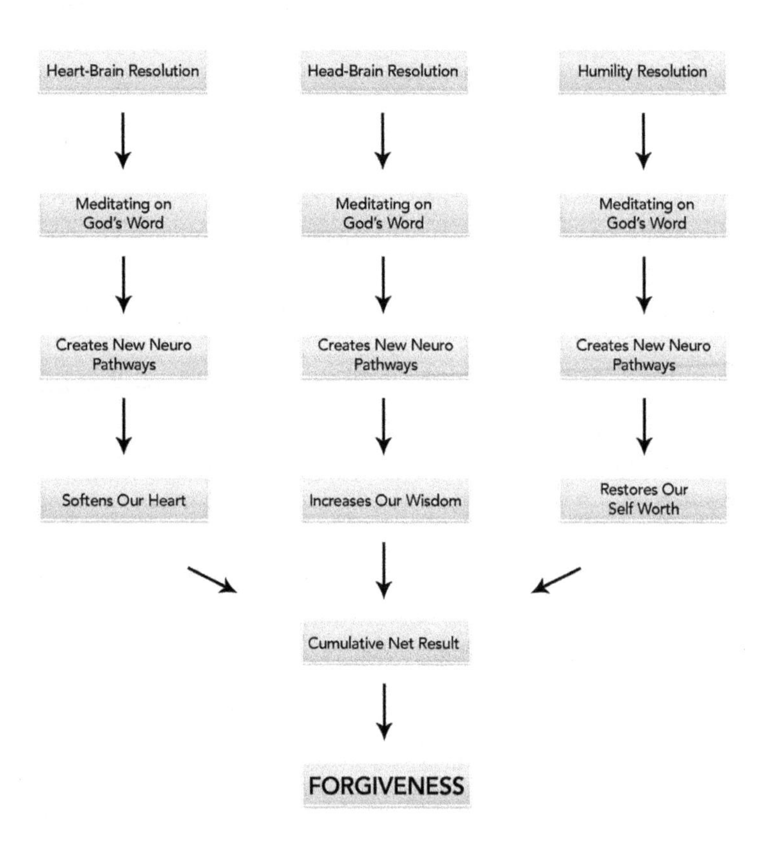

Chapter Nine

Unlocking the Physiological Benefits of Renewing Our Minds (Living a Godly Life)

Thank you for pushing forward through the foundational part of the book! Now we can begin to unlock the overwhelming beauty, love, and simplicity of living life God's way. I do not think there is a person on this earth who does not want to be healthy, wealthy, and wise. Okay, I can hear some of you saying, "well, maybe I have one or two of those qualities, but can anyone *really* have all three?"

Absolutely, but there is a caveat! "There is always the proverbial fine print, isn't there?" you can say jokingly. Seriously, the only limitation is the degree to which we have "renewed" our mind. Think of it this way: if we could push a button and instantly overwrite our brain with all God's precepts and wisdom, we would live in perfect health, everything we put our hands to would prosper because we would be all-knowing. The net result would be a person whose body is in a constant state of rest!

Here is the Biblical confirmation that God truly wants us to be healthy, wealthy, and wise.

> "For I know the plans and thoughts that I have for you," says the Lord, "plans for peace and well-being and not for disaster, to give you a future and a hope."
>
> Jeremiah 29:11 (AMP)

> Blessed [fortunate, prosperous, and favored by God] is the man who does not walk in the counsel of the wicked [following their advice and example], Nor stand in the path of sinners, Nor sit [down to rest] in the seat of scoffers (ridiculers).
>
> Psalm 1:1 (AMP)

> But the humble will [at last] inherit the land And will delight themselves in abundant prosperity and peace.
>
> Psalm 37:11 (AMP)

> He who pays attention to the word [of God] will find good, And blessed (happy, prosperous, to be admired) is he who trusts [confidently] in the Lord.
>
> Proverbs 16:20 (AMP)

Chapter Summary

This chapter can be summed up in the following single biblical passage. Remember: use your Spiritual Eyes...do not just read the Bible; you must READ the Bible.

> My son, pay attention to my words and be willing to learn; Open your ears to my sayings. Do not let them escape from your sight; Keep them in the center of your heart. For they are life to those who find them, And healing and health to all their flesh.
>
> Proverbs 4:20-22 (AMP)

My sincere hope and purpose of all the previous foundation information were to give you the ability to see this verse from a different perspective. In case it does not jump off the page for you, I will break it down, piece by piece, to expose the underlying physiology.

"My son, pay attention to my words and be willing to learn; Open your ears to my sayings." A person who is willing to learn is a humble person whose ears are open (in this case) to hear God's wisdom and suggestions on how to live, the "humility resolution." Remember, being Spiritually humble is one of the three ingredients necessary to forgive people and remove bitterness (a bitter person is consumed with stress and anxiety).

"Do not let them escape from your sight" speaks to the second ingredient necessary to forgive people and remove bitterness (a bitter person is consumed with stress and anxiety), the "head-brain" resolution. To not let God's Word escape from our sight requires us to read His Word continually, which is performed by our brain. It creates new neuropathways associated with the wisdom of God.

"Keep them in the center of your heart" speaks to the third ingredient necessary to forgive people and remove bitterness (a bitter person is consumed with stress and anxiety), the "heart-brain" resolution. It is not enough to just have head knowledge (His Words in our brain). God is telling us to also write His Words in our heart! Writing to our heart means the creation of new neuropathways within the heart.

"For they are life to those who find them, And healing and health to all their flesh." As I have mentioned a number of times, God's Word is life-breathed and proof that the Bible is not a compilation of stories written by a man. His Words change our entire physiology. They can heal all our wounds and change our beliefs, leading to a healthy genetic output for all of our flesh (every cell, every organ)!

Epilogue

All the Glory to Him! It is my sincere hope that you do not see "me" after reading this book. The only claim I can honestly make is that I typed the words. If you would like to comment on this book, you can do so on my website: alltheglorytohim.com. By way of example, have you ever gone online to purchase an image? In order to be able to use a picture taken by someone other than yourself, you must pay a licensing fee. In essence, the person who took the picture (original owner) will give you the right to use that picture.

In the very same way, I am only a vehicle being used by the Holy Spirit to convey a picture to you. I am licensed but could *never* lay claim to being the originator of the wisdom!

To me, the miracle of this book is the irony of the preverbal question of where we came from, creation or evolution? On the one hand, most scientists today are still trying to use their discoveries to validate evolution but are unknowingly proving that all we see with our eyes had to be created by intelligence. For me, it is as simple as this! The big bang theory, which is based on an explosion, could never produce beauty. Think about it: we have all seen explosions (the bombs of war); did any of those explosions create beauty? No, they ripped the beauty of our world apart!

As I stated previously, it is only in the past ten years that science discovered enough information about how our brain functions to enable the understanding and depth of what God has been saying all along, "My Way is the only way if you want to be healthy, wealthy and wise."

Think about that for more than just a minute. God's Word has been around for more than 6,000 years, yet only until recently can we peer into the underlying physiological meanings and benefits of living life His Way.

There is a huge difference between knowing about God and being in a relationship with God! Relationships are based on *trust*. Trusting in God (ultimately, that is all He ever wanted) is synonymous with having *faith*. For most of the past 6,000 years, without the science to validate what God has been saying, it took *faith* to believe in all the promises of God.

Over the past 6,000 years, several people have dedicated their lives to identifying all of the promises found in the Bible. The word "promise" appears over 100 times in the Bible, and thousands more are listed in Samuel Clarke's two-hundred-year-old classic, Precious Bible Promises. These promises are centered around seven main categories.

- I will be with you
- I will protect you
- I will be your strength
- I will answer you
- I will provide for you
- I will give you peace
- I will always be with you

In my second book, I will show you beyond any shadow of a doubt, the scientific proof of how the promises of God's Word can change our physiology.

Overview: The person whose mind is shaped by the world's viewpoints and ways of thinking is consumed with self-absorption, anger, hatred, vengeance, stress, anxiety, fear, and unforgiveness. All of which are thieves robbing us of the energy we need to make changes in our life. God says we need to remove our unforgiveness (bitterness) first to energize ourselves, freeing us up to begin the process of renewing our minds.

To effectively renew our mind with God's precepts and wisdom, we must *read* His Word repetitively, actively meditate on what we have read (keep it in the forefront of our mind), and speak it out aloud just like we did when we were learning the times table. This is the process that creates new neuropathways and generates a *new* voice in our mind. God's voice!

The more we rehearse the process of repetition, mediation, and speaking, the greater our discernment of who is speaking to us will be. Our new Godly voice will begin to change our thoughts, feelings, emotions. These changes will eventually alter our belief system. When our beliefs change from negative beliefs to positive beliefs, our genetic output changes, producing a healthy body chemistry.

Key point: we learned a great deal of information, and I want to make sure you did not miss the central theme. The central theme was that living without a Godly renewed mind leads to a life full of stress, anxiety, and fear. Until I did all this research, I had no clue how much stress, anxiety, and fear destroy our health. I will be providing extensive details regarding these destroyers of health in my next book, Biblical Nutrition.

My second book, *Biblical Nutrition*, will be centered around the following verse. Try to read this one on your own. In case you do not see it...I will be breaking it down in the beginning of the second book.

> Do not be anxious or worried about anything, but in everything [every circumstance and situation] by prayer and petition with thanksgiving, continue to make your [specific] requests known to God. And the peace of God [that peace which reassures the heart, that peace] which transcends all understanding, [that peace which] stands guard over your hearts and your minds in Christ Jesus [is yours].
>
> Philippians 4:6-7 (AMP)

About the Author

I have spent many hours contemplating what to say about myself. I realized that elaborating on myself would only redirect your focus from being in a relationship with God, Jesus, and Holy Spirit on to me. Seeing me...is not important.

It is sufficient to say I have experienced many of the same life's ups and downs as you have, even going so far as to die. As the saying goes, "been to hell and back" more times than I care to remember. What I truly hope I conveyed to you by writing this book and the ones to follow is the heart, love, and wisdom God has towards us.

With all the lack of our understanding of how the human mind works, it amazes me how the loving heart of God still figured out the exact Words we needed to hear to transition us from impulsive habitual creatures seeking after speechless idols into mature Spiritual beings full of love for God and one another.

For, it is my heart's desire that by writing this book, I might expedite your transition. To that extent, the greatest piece of wisdom I can share with you would be to seek and pray to the Holy Spirit. During the beginning of my transition, I prayed to God and Jesus as I had been taught. As I continued my walk with God, Jesus, and the Holy Spirit, I noticed a pattern.

The Holy Spirit directed my attention to the scriptures about Him. I leave you with the following verses to read:

> So then, brothers and sisters, we have an obligation, but not to our flesh [our human nature, our worldliness, our sinful capacity], to live according to the [impulses of the] flesh [our nature without the Holy Spirit]—for if you are living according to the [impulses of the] flesh, you are going to die. But if [you are living] by the [power of the Holy] Spirit you are habitually putting to death the sinful deeds of the body, you will [really] live forever. For all who are allowing themselves to be led by the Spirit of God are sons of God.
>
> Romans 8:12-14 (AMP)

> The [reverent] fear of the Lord [that is, worshiping Him and regarding Him as truly awesome] is the beginning and the preeminent part of wisdom [its starting point and its essence], And the knowledge of the Holy One is understanding and spiritual insight.
>
> Proverbs 9:10 (AMP)

> But I tell you the truth, it is to your advantage that I go away; for if I do not go away, the Helper (Comforter, Advocate, Intercessor—Counselor, Strengthener, Standby) will not come to you; but if I go, I will send Him (the Holy Spirit) to you [to be in close fellowship with you].
>
> John 16:7 (AMP)

> But the Helper (Comforter, Advocate, Intercessor—Counselor, Strengthener, Standby), the Holy Spirit, whom the Father will send in My name [in My place, to represent Me and act on My behalf], He will teach you all things. And He will help you remember everything that I have told you.
>
> John 14:26 (AMP)

> But the fruit of the Spirit [the result of His presence within us] is love [unselfish concern for others], joy, [inner] peace, patience [not the ability to wait, but how we act while waiting], kindness, goodness, faithfulness, gentleness, self-control. Against such things there is no law.
>
> Galatians 5:22-23 (AMP)

Thank you for your time and consideration! My second book will be out in the fall of 2021. Until then, begin your walk by substituting your name into this scripture every time you read the word "you/your."

—Blessings, Rick

For this reason [grasping the greatness of this plan by which Jews and Gentiles are joined together in Christ] I bow my knees [in reverence] before the Father [of our Lord Jesus Christ], from whom every family in heaven and on earth derives its name [God—the first and ultimate Father]. May He grant you out of the riches of His glory, to be strengthened and spiritually energized with power through His Spirit in your inner self, [indwelling your innermost being and personality], so that Christ may dwell in your hearts through your faith. And may you, having been [deeply] rooted and [securely] grounded in love, be fully capable of comprehending with all the saints (God's people) the width and length and height and depth of His love [fully experiencing that amazing, endless love]; and [that you may come] to know [practically, through personal experience] the love of Christ which far surpasses [mere] knowledge [without experience], that you may be filled up [throughout your being] to all the fullness of God [so that you may have the richest experience of God's presence in your lives, completely filled and flooded with God Himself].

Now to Him who is able to [carry out His purpose and] do superabundantly more than all that we dare ask or think [infinitely beyond our greatest prayers, hopes, or dreams], according to His power that is at work within us, to Him be the glory in the church and in Christ Jesus throughout all generations forever and ever. Amen.

Ephesians 3:14-21 (AMP)

Endnotes

Chapter One

1 "About Dr. Leaf," website, https://drleaf.com/pages/about-dr-leaf

Chapter Five

2 Wikipedia, "United States incarceration rate" entry.

Chapter Six

3 Annette Capps, *Quantum Faith* (Harrison House Publishers, 2006), 11-12.

4 Capps, *Quantum Faith*, 6–7.

5 Capps, *Quantum Faith*, 1.

6 Capps, *Quantum Faith*, 7–8.

7 Capps, *Quantum Faith*, 9.

8 Capps, *Quantum Faith*, 13–14.

9 Capps, *Quantum Faith*, 14.

Chapter Seven

10 Wikipedia, "Discernment" entry, "Christian Spiritual Discernment" section.

11 "The Neuron," BrainFacts.Org, last reviewed April 1, 2012, www.brainfacts.org/brain-anatomy-and-function/anatomy/2012/the-neuron

12 "New Estimate Boosts the Human Brain's Memory Capacity 10-Fold" by Jeneen Interlandi, *Scientific American*, published February 5, 2016, www.scientificamerican.com/article/new-estimate-boosts-the-human-brain-s-memory-capacity-10-fold

13 "Plasticity in Neural Networks," The Brain from Top to Bottom, https://thebrain.mcgill.ca/flash/d/d_07/d_07_cl/d_07_cl_tra/d_07_cl_tra.html

14 "Synapses," The Brain from Top to Bottom, https://thebrain.mcgill.ca/flash/i/i_01/i_01_m/i_01_m_ana/i_01_m_ana.html

15 Wikipedia, "Essential amino acid" entry.

Chapter Eight

16 "The Negative Effects of Unforgiveness on Mental Health," Theravive, April 28, 2014, https://www.theravive.com/today/post/the-negative-effects-of-unforgiveness-on-mental-health-0001467.aspx

17 "5 Reasons You're not Helping Yourself by Reading Self-Help Books, and How to Actually Improve Your Life" by Matthew Jones, March 28, 2016, https://thoughtcatalog.com/matthew-jones/2016/03/5-reasons-youre-not-helping-yourself-by-reading-self-help-books-and-how-to-actually-improve-your-life/

18 "The Origins and Evolution of Epigenetics" by Ute Deichmann, Developmental Biology Volume 416, Issue 1, August, 1 2016, 249-254.

19 Wikipedia, "Bruce Lipton" entry, "Biography" section.

20 Wikipedia, "Quantum entanglement" entry.

21 "Let Your Heart Talk to Your Brain" by Deborah Rozman, HuffPost, updated December 6, 2017, https://www.huffpost.com/entry/heart-wisdom_b_2615857

22 Wikipedia, "Humility" entry.

23 Wikipedia, "Humility" entry, "Religious views of humility" section, Judaism subsection.

CPSIA information can be obtained
at www.ICGtesting.com
Printed in the USA
LVHW081342230621
R16818900001B/R168189PG690796LVX00001B/1

9 781637 690208